90 DAYS TO SUCCESS AS A MANAGER

Anthony T. Meola

WITHDRAWN

Course Technology PTR
A part of Cengage Learning

COURSE TECHNOLOGY
CENGAGE Learning™

Australia, Brazil, Japan, Korea, Mexico, Singapore, Spain, United Kingdom, United States

COURSE TECHNOLOGY
CENGAGE Learning™

90 Days to Success as a Manager
Anthony T. Meola

Publisher and General Manager, Course Technology PTR:
Stacy L. Hiquet

Associate Director of Marketing:
Sarah Panella

Manager of Editorial Services:
Heather Talbot

Marketing Manager:
Mark Hughes

Acquisitions Editor:
Mitzi Koontz

Project Editor/Copy Editor:
Cathleen D. Small

Editorial Services Coordinator:
Jen Blaney

Interior Layout Tech:
Bill Hartman

Cover Designer:
Luke Fletcher

Indexer:
Larry Sweazy

Proofreader:
Heather Urschel

For product information and technology assistance, contact us at **Cengage Learning Customer & Sales Support, 1-800-354-9706**

For permission to use material from this text or product, submit all requests online at **cengage.com/permissions** Further permissions questions can be e-mailed to **permissionrequest@cengage.com**.

All trademarks are the property of their respective owners.

Library of Congress Control Number: 2008935221

ISBN-13: 978-1-59863-865-3

ISBN-10: 1-59863-865-3

Course Technology, a part of Cengage Learning
20 Channel Center Street
Boston, MA 02210
USA

Cengage Learning is a leading provider of customized learning solutions with office locations around the globe, including Singapore, the United Kingdom, Australia, Mexico, Brazil, and Japan. Locate your local office at: **international.cengage.com/region**.

Cengage Learning products are represented in Canada by Nelson Education, Ltd.

For your lifelong learning solutions, visit **courseptr.com**.

Visit our corporate Web site at **cengage.com**.

Printed in Canada
2 3 4 5 6 7 11 10 09

To my wife, Marian, who was with me every step of the way throughout my career and always supported me. I could not have accomplished any of this without her by my side. To my children, Matt, Greg, and Lindsay, who all contributed in their own way and made their own sacrifices that contributed to their Dad's success. And to everyone who took a moment to give an inquisitive kid a piece of advice along the way—thank you all.

Acknowledgments

It's been said over and over again that we are to an extent a product of our environment. The people we meet and who influence us along the way make up our personal environment, and I am no exception to that rule. There are so many people I would like to acknowledge who helped me along the way that, frankly, it is an impossible task, but there are a few that I would like to mention to say a special thanks, because they stood out in some way in my mind, and I reflect on their words even today.

To begin with, there is my immediate family. My wife, Marian, has been by my side for the whole journey and has always been a source of inspiration and confidence. My kids, Matt, Greg, and Lindsay, have been my motivation and my joy in life.

Then there was my family that I grew up with—my mother, my brother, Tom, and my sister, Terri. Being the youngest in a family where our father had passed away at an early age, they all *made sure* they took care of me. I learned from all of them so many things, but my work ethic, my values, and my passion for doing the right thing come from them.

When I got out into the world, there were the people I worked for who took an interest in me, such as Rich Guerry at Amerada Hess and Frank Bevaqua at Citicorp, who both taught me so much about discipline in operations and precision in management and how to hold people accountable.

Every successful manager always has a mentor, and mine was and is a gentleman named Sy Naqvi. Sy is simply the most brilliant manager I have ever met. He taught me to always think about the implications of one's actions. He also introduced me to an executive coach, Deborah Allen Baber, who he chose specifically for me, and she really helped me to understand and think strategically about things.

And finally there is my father-in-law, Fred Pelaia. He was my "agent in life"; he gave me the confidence to step into larger roles throughout my career and the nudge we all need sometimes to take the plunge—and thanks to him, I did!

And finally, to the countless people I have met in my career who have said to me, "You know, Tony, you should write a book."

About the Author

Anthony T. Meola was born in Newark, New Jersey, and was raised in nearby Bloomfield with his brother and sister. His mother valued education, having been one of the few women of her time to earn a college degree, and when she was widowed at a young age, she made certain she passed that value to her children. Tony attended Rutgers University on an academic scholarship and completed his degree in three years. He joined Amerada Hess as an entry-level accountant and quickly moved through the organization, becoming one of its youngest controllers in its history. After seven years with Hess, Tony joined Citibank, where he continued his success, becoming the chief financial officer of its mortgage company after four years with the organization. He later became an executive vice president of the bank's Loan Servicing Division and ran its telemarketing operation for first mortgages. He left Citibank to become PNC Mortgage Company's chief operations officer, and he later became its head of all production operations and eventually the chief operating officer. Known as a problem solver in the financial services industry, Tony was asked to stay on and join Washington Mutual's Executive Leadership team as the director of loan servicing and consumer direct business after WaMu's acquisition of PNC Mortgage. Eventually, he would become the co-head of Mortgage Business. His accomplishments at WaMu included partnering with Earvin Johnson and Johnson Development Corporation to bring financial services and home loans to underserved communities, as well as forming the largest single-platform mortgage servicer at the time, through consolidating and merging various companies' technological platforms, processes, and cultures.

Today, Tony is the CEO of Morgan Stanley's U.S. residential business, where he is responsible for all aspects of Morgan Stanley's Business Strategy and Operational Execution in the mortgage space for the United States. He is a recognized industry leader in the mortgage industry and has served on the Mortgage Bankers Association's Residential Board of Governors. He has also served on the Board of the Chicago Public Education Fund and is involved in public speaking and executive coaching. He resides in Barrington, Illinois, with his wife, Marian, and daughter, Lindsay. He also has two sons, Matt, a University of Michigan graduate, and Greg, a graduate of Holy Cross College.

Contents

Introduction

I think the last thing the world needs right now is another management book. Believe me, I have read a ton of them over the years and still have yet to find one that mattered to me in a way that changed something about me. Don't get me wrong: There are a number of good books on the topic—a large number at that—but I always looked for one that would make me aware of the changes I needed to make to become a better manager. A book written by a real manager with real experiences and lessons learned that I could relate to, understand, and reflect on—one that gave me some things to think about and some tools to perfect my style with, and one that would actually make me a better manager.

Think about that: Imagine if you could actually read a book that would make you a better manager than you are right now. What would that do for your company, for the people you manage, and most of all for you?!

That's the book I wanted to read, so I challenged myself to write it.

I have been fortunate to have had the opportunity to know some great mentors over the years, and I have always been someone who is an observer of life and who learns from those observations. I was always taught that smart people learn from their mistakes, but smarter people learn from other people's mistakes, so I always viewed things from that perspective. I would always ask—and still do—what can I or did I learn from this and how do I become better?

With that approach and 30 years in the business world, I have collected a number of best practices and perfected a number more. In this book I try to relate those experiences in actionable learnings that can help you become a better manager. The 90-day part is simple—either you are going to change some things by simply becoming aware of them and making them part of your style or you are not. But if you do, you will begin to see and feel the results of a new management approach that will actually work and be enjoyable.

You won't see a bibliography in this book. I didn't do academic research; there are libraries filled with management books that will explain the technical terms of management and give you the Ivy League vocabulary to speak eloquently and pointedly on any management topic you need. My frame of reference for this book was the last 30 years of managing people, being in large organizations and observing behaviors, and, with all humility, succeeding at it.

You can say what you want about the formulae, but it took a poor kid from Newark, New Jersey, to the ranks of a CEO, so there must be something to it! I can tell you this: Had I known then what I have learned since, the ride would have been much faster and so much smoother.

I manage a large number of people today and speak to an even larger number about managing. I love it! I have a passion for developing managers, and I believe that management can really make or—as we have seen so recently in our economy—break a company.

Let's face it: All companies have processes, technologies, policies, and procedures. In fact, all companies have people as well, and some have the same strategy and approach to the market. So, how does one company beat another in the marketplace?

I believe the answer is its leadership and, more importantly, how that leadership manages—how it navigates the market, reacts, responds, creates the environment for its employees to perform, recognizes change, and brings about change. Ask any executive, and he or she will tell you that what you don't have in strategy, you make up in execution. Execution is the cornerstone of a company's success, and it's the company's managers who are responsible for execution.

The problem is that management development is generally not a core competency of organizations. They'll have some training programs, and the better ones will have a leadership development program, but these are usually textbook-oriented, with very few practical life experiences. Even when practical experience is introduced through a speaker or through an exercise, it rarely is something the attendees take back and implement. Why that's the case I cannot say for certain, but I believe it is because of the way these things are communicated that they do not connect for the managers.

What you are about to read is a book that will make the connections for you with real-life experiences. It will provide you with a frame of reference of a successful manager. As you read the book, you will adopt some of the philosophies; others you will not, and some you will modify as you internalize them, but you will think about all of them, I can assure you.

That is the beauty of being a manager—it is the personal skill that you develop every day of consuming input, data, and knowledge and then taking action. There is room for creativity and individualism, which makes managers unique, but management is both art and science, and that is why one must work at it and have an approach and a style of executing it with a certain balance of flare and precision.

It is my hope that managers who read this book will simply think about its topics and form their own style and approach to managing in a conscious way. If they utilize these suggestions and become better managers, that would be a wonderful thing, but if all this book does is cause them to think about how they are managing, then frankly it has achieved its goal, because they will become better managers for having thought about it.

Chapter 1

Vision, Mission, and Values

- Where Are You Going?
- Creating Your Vision
- Refining Your Vision
- Holding onto Your Vision
- Your Mission Statement
- Your Values

Congratulations! You are a manager of a department. So you may be asking yourself, "Now what?" Well, you are about to go on a journey—it's called "your career in management," and if you are like most managers, you haven't had much preparation or training for this moment. Managing is like anything else: The better you prepare yourself, the more likely you are to be successful. You need to think about your career as a journey, because that is exactly what it is. It twists and turns and presents many roads for you to follow—different paths, and all of them (yes, all of them) can lead to success.

Where Are You Going?

First you must decide where you want to go.

The first part of any journey starts with a question formed by two simple words: Where to? Before you begin interacting, read your first report, dive into the first big issue, interview a single person, or talk to your boss about how it's going so far, you need to understand where you want to go by thinking about questions such as:

- What do you want to accomplish?
- Where do you want to lead this department?
- How will you operate?
- What will your department be known for a year from now?
- What will you be known for a year from now?
- What will people say about the results you have accomplished?
- And what will those results be, exactly?

When people talk about you and your management style, what will they say about you to your peers, your employees, your boss, and even your family and friends? Regardless of whether you just became a manager today or you are an established manager who is looking for advice to break out and become a great one, you will answer each one of those questions by your actions and behavior throughout your time in management.

Establishing Your True North

Find your true north: Define your own vision of where you want you and your team to be.

Regardless of your experience level, it is time to tackle taking aim of your own vision of where you want you and your team to be. Make a plan to get there, and then relentlessly pursue that plan, adjust it, mold it, nurture it, and do something every day to get there. I call it *establishing your true north*.

The direction you decide to go is based on your own personal value system, what you want to become, and where you can lead your people. Once you are in touch with that, and you relate it back to your role in the company and in your career, then you are truly a successful manager. It is easier said than done, but worth the investment in time and effort.

Here is your first step in the process of becoming a great manager: Write down for yourself, as detailed as you can, what your vision is for your department. For example, if you were running training, you might say something like, "Our department will be known for productivity improvement. People will say, 'Get training in here; they know how to increase productivity—they are experts!'"

Your first step should be to write down what your vision is for your department.

If that is your vision, you then need to consider how to bring that about. Managing is about people, process, and technology. You select people, train them, give them tools, and then manage them every day to achieve the goal. Suppose your vision is to have a training department that people would be in awe of because of the results you enable people to achieve after they have been trained by your team. If that is your true north, then you must commit to it above all other outcomes. This thought process this approach of relentless commitment to a defined goal—will impact everything you do. You can envision how it will effect your course selection, the people you hire, how you train them, how you prioritize tasks, the technology you use, how you measure your success, and the skill sets you choose to develop in your people. It will dictate what you spend your time and money on and even how you discuss issues and conduct yourself.

Managing is about people, process, and technology.

Under this scenario, would you pay 10 percent over a job grade for a trainer who was regarded as one of the best in the industry? It is a pretty easy answer. If your vision were instead to be the lowest-cost provider of training in your space, then you might think twice about the pay-up. You might still do it, but you can feel the difference in the decision process, can't you? That is the power of vision. So before you engage in something so powerful, you need to make certain you have it right. It becomes a requirement for you to understand the expectations of those around you and those who placed you in this role.

A meeting with your boss, your peer group, and anyone else who has relevant interest and influence in your area is in order as step one. You need to ask the questions that will ultimately define your success and your people's success.

- What do you want from this area?
- What does success look like to you for this area?
- What would be the single biggest accomplishment you believe you could bring about in this area?

These are the questions you need to ask all your constituents that will determine your success—your boss, your employees, and your auditors and peer groups.

The most important thing is to find out what your customers want.

Most important is to find out what your customers want. Customer surveys are an open-book test. If your company tracks the "internal customer," while not always a smart approach (there is only one customer—but that's a different book), it will serve you well in understanding your departmental interactions.

Understanding the Data

Find the common themes and the top priorities, and then discuss these with your boss and your employees.

After you collect all the data inputs, it's time to sort out the common themes, the top priorities you see, and then "lock and load" with your boss and your employees to understand whether you heard what they said and prioritized it appropriately. In two weeks' time, you should have formed the external success factors for your department and learned from your employees the things that would allow them to be successful and, more importantly, feel successful.

Spend time with all the data you collect, understand it, clarify it, and keep a record of it. You will need to refer to it; it will help you make the tough decisions and enable you to get through the tough times. These conversations will define the dragon that you will slay and will be the very success you achieve.

Creating Your Vision

Now and only now are you ready to create your vision. You have heard from everyone about what they believe you should do, and maybe even how to do it, but you have all the data points, so now you need to draw the line that will define you.

Create for yourself the vision. Don't get wrapped around trying to come up with a statement; first just write as much as you can and want to about how your department will look, feel, and operate and the results it will achieve under your leadership.

Create your vision and boil it down to a simple but powerful statement.

From that, boil it down to a simple but powerful statement. Here's an example: "We will provide service that will be recognized as a competitive advantage by our customers, co-workers, competitors, and the marketplace at large."

You can feel the power of the vision statement, but more importantly, it is a call to action. Think about how this vision statement affects how you manage. Who you select, what tools you invest in, the procedures you write, the processes you create...they will all be aligned in one goal—creating service that is an advantage. With this vision, if your competition solves customer issues in 48 hours, then you must do it in less time. Your vision will dictate your actions. If employee satisfaction correlates, as studies suggest, to customer satisfaction, then you will create a highly desirable workplace. You may be a low-cost provider because that creates a competitive advantage, but you won't sacrifice service to do it with this vision. When done correctly, a vision statement creates clarity and purpose and becomes a guide for the manager.

Your vision will dictate your actions.

Your vision statement will guide you in your role as manager, so it must be clear and purposeful.

Suppose you manage accounts payable; what would your vision be? Accounts payable can earn money for the company by taking advantage of early pay discounts, and it can provide insight by properly recording expenses so that managers see the impact of spending. It can provide reports on major expense items to highlight them, and it can see trends that others can't. It can keep services flowing and vendors engaged. A vision statement for accounts payable might read like this: "Provide payment processing that creates information to better our company," or "Process payments efficiently and intelligently."

People want to work for someone with a vision; they also want to be part of something. You don't need a fancy trinket or T-shirt with your department's vision—leave that for the company. What you *do* need is to have a clear vision, let your people know it, and then work to bring it about.

People want to work for someone with a vision.

I once was given the responsibility of running a large customer service organization. After doing some homework and talking to many people at all levels, including peer groups, bosses, and employees, and reading customer data, it became clear to me that the organization was very slow to respond to inquiries and never initiated contact. Furthermore, because of inadequate staffing, they were difficult to do business with. They were short on the phone, defensive, and antagonistic. They were downright mean—to customers, each other, and everyone they dealt with!

I had a vision for this group that they would be known someday by all who encountered them as proactive, responsive, and friendly to do business with. They would be known as the best area for service in the company, and they would be an advantage upon which our sales force would sell.

Slowly and painfully, the transformation began. We hired new people to a profile of proactive, responsive, and friendly. We trained the workforce differently. We provided tools that would allow one-stop resolution; we broke the mold and hierarchy that existed to enable our people to reach out to customers, departments, and management.

We changed the way centers were configured. The art on the walls came down, and our own advertisements, internal banners, and metrics went up in their place. We changed the way we rated people to actually rate and give performance feedback around being proactive, responsive, and friendly.

We invested in technology that better routed calls to subject-matter experts, we scripted our call centers with friendly greetings, we encouraged customer conversations, and we sent out communications to our sales force on good and bad trends that we were experiencing in providing service. We gave high-fives, we had huddle meetings, we let people know what was happening every morning, and we celebrated the achievements of that vision every time it happened. The energy in the place soared; we became proud of our ability to respond, we got out in front of issues and kept people informed, we took pride in the fact that we satisfied customers the first time, and we actually began to track repeat calls. If you're responsive, you should never have a repeat call, should you?

That's the power of a vision. But it succeeded beyond the obvious; the organization operated more effectively. Why? Because fewer mistakes meant fewer inquiries—proactive took on a different meaning. Our customer satisfaction soared 60 percentage points, from 32 percent of our customers satisfied to 92 percent satisfied; our costs lowered over time with less rework needed; and people enjoyed their jobs. In the end, we helped our organization, ourselves, and our customers because we had a vision. It took 36 months to achieve that vision, but everyone to this very day who was part of that organization remembers it as one of the highest performance environments and most fun places they ever worked.

Vision is defining where you want to be in the future and then having a plan that gets you there.

I have taken on a number of turnaround situations in my career, from departments to companies and even in volunteer organizations. In all these experiences, it has consistently amazed me that the one issue each failed situation had in common was a lack of vision. Vision isn't a hope or dream; rather, it is truly visualizing yourself in the future and then having a plan that gets you there. That is the difference—having a plan that gets you there. That requires thought. The more you think about your vision and the more you talk about it, the greater chance you will achieve it. You need to enlist everyone around you and not be afraid to share your vision so that others can pick it up and carry it forward. Sometimes they can move your vision better than you can, and that is all right—in fact, it is preferred. You have heard the Chinese proverb, "Give a man a fish and you feed him for a day. Teach a man to fish and you feed him for a lifetime." That is true leadership.

Refining Your Vision

Visions can and do change; they are sometimes altered by fact, external changes, and time. Most of the time, they are molded and perfected, but the core principles remain the same. They are always challenged and always doubted, and they always take time to be understood and accepted. Don't let resistance be a negative factor in your vision. Use it to mold your vision! The key is knowing when and what to hold onto, and to hold tightly to those aspects that simply define the vision. No cost is greater than giving up what you have envisioned once you have gone through the process of creating a vision.

Visions change— they are molded and perfected, but the core remains unchanged.

I once had an assignment to turn an entire company around. It had been a small company, owner-led for most of its existence, and now it found itself part of a large corporation with a huge growth potential. The problem was it was incapable of growth! Its systems, processes, and procedures were not scalable, but that was only part of the issue. The biggest challenge that company faced was that its people were not scalable. They had grown up

Instead of letting resistance to your vision be a negative factor, use it to further mold your vision!

in a company that did most of the thinking for them, even at the most senior level, and their approaches and skills were honed to a small-company environment. The senior team didn't engage in management unless something was broken—and even then all they would do is conduct a fire drill to fix things, followed by asking who was to blame. If nothing went wrong in the course of a day, then there was no work or interaction unless the boss had an idea—that was the extent of the activity.

What they did, they did well—their business was fairly good, and they only took on so much. No one pushed the envelope, and no one dared to change a process or improve one. When the market changed, however, their company began to fail and eventually was purchased. That's when I got a call to come and "make it scalable."

I started with interviews of management, auditors, and employees and customer survey information asking a simple question: What does a great company look like that has scale? That led to a second and more important question: What does it mean to be scalable? I conducted interviews and focus groups with these questions, supplemented by a "what's working and what's not working" session.

The entire data-gathering process took 45 days. More importantly, I got to meet all of the key constituents who impacted the organization and the employees whose mission it would be to carry out this vision. I received all their input and gave them a chance to tell me their perspective on the challenges ahead of us all. In the "what's working and what's not working" sessions, I got to feel the emotions and passions of the employee base. I heard what was important to them and, frankly, what was not. I also learned the best ways to communicate with them—a lesson that is valuable under any circumstances.

Out of those sessions came a vision, and oddly enough, it had little to do with the specifics of scalability! Don't misunderstand me—scalability was a part of what that vision was, but it was not the core, and it was not the heartbeat of the vision.

What I quickly learned in my discussions with senior management was that scalability was a key component of something bigger, something that the most senior management of the organization had in mind for this small company they had purchased. They wanted to create value—in other words, worth. A value they could retain or market or sell. But the bottom line was that they perceived that in a turbulent and volatile market, when the dust settled, they could have a business in this sector that was well run, executed in a best-in-class manner, and could grow to be valuable. So the vision was born: Create value!

Holding onto Your Vision

There is a saying, "To thine own self be true." There is nothing more important and more difficult than holding true to a vision, but then again, there is nothing like the feeling you will experience when you realize that vision—nothing!

Management is about resources—that is what you manage. That is the role of a manager: deploying resources, gathering resources, mobilizing resources, and enabling resources to achieve a goal. Resources come in two varieties: human and capital. That means you need to define your vision across those two axes. And if management is also about people, process, and technology, then you must hold fast to your vision across these as well, which can be taxing even in the best of times.

Management is about human and capital resources.

People are a tough resource to manage under any conditions, but when you are taking over an organization, a department, or a unit—whether it's 10, 20, or 20,000 people—they will need to adapt themselves to the vision. Some will not, and they may have been—and maybe currently are—technically capable, maybe even the best in class for the past environment. Some may be your top managers, best performers, and long-tenure employees.

The challenge here is bring those people with you into the new world. If they assimilate into it, they will be just as successful as they always have been, but if they don't—if they can't or if they simply don't believe in your vision—then you must let them go. The faster you make that decision, generally the better it is for everyone—namely, you, them, and all the people who surround you both.

When you take over a department or an organization, people will need to adapt to the vision. If they cannot (or will not), you must be prepared to let them go.

Remember, it is difficult for people who have been successful in their career or even in their own mind to adapt. I use the word *adapt* versus *change* because people don't change in a metamorphic way when they are in their 20s, 30s, and 40s, and that is what your workforce demographic is. They do adapt, though, and the difference is that adaptation is modifying your behavior to fit an environment for a different purpose, while change is actually making your behavior different. Very few people will be made different by you, but many can internalize your message into their self-being and act upon it.

You must begin to manage to your vision, reinforce it through recognition, and reward the behaviors and attributes of your vision. I once conducted a personnel review with a set of managers who spoke to me about the performance of all their direct reports. In that review, a manager made a statement that one of his team members was a "great" performer, probably one of the best technical managers he had ever come across, and certainly best in class in his discipline. His weakness was that he was a terrible team player, and often his style alienated people. He really didn't value teamwork.

The problem here was that the vision included the statement, "We will work as a team," and we were in a business that required communications across lines for us to be effective. You see the dilemma? What would you have done? We fired him. Would you have done the same?

Give people a chance to commit to your vision and recognize when someone will adapt and when they will not.

You must be relentless in the commitment to your vision and give people a chance to join in, but also recognize as soon as possible in the process when someone will adapt and when the issue is hopeless. Frankly, if people are not against what you are trying to accomplish but may not know yet how to partake in it, then they are for it, and you must figure out how to engage them. That's the job of a manager.

I was part of a team that had the vision "efficiency with quality," and that team faced a dilemma in that they operated with outdated systems, which meant they had many manual processes that required long hours—lots of overtime. They had a strong leader; she had a parental style, and they loved her—it was a "family," and they referred to it as such.

A new system would improve the quality of the work: With automated checks and balances, it would speed the process through workflows, and it would reduce staff and eliminate overtime. Do you see the dilemma? A new system would destroy the "family." So, the question became are you committed to the vision or to the "family"? Management is not easy—commitment to a vision means making decisions along the way that are not only difficult to make, but that are gut wrenching.

Decisions like this impact people's lives, but remember this: Decisions impact *all* people's lives, not just the ones that may be impacted negatively. In this example, if we didn't employ a new system, we would have been less competitive and less profitable, and our company would not have returned to its investors its full potential. Eventually we might have gone out of business for cost reasons. What about those "families"?

Commitment to a vision means making decisions that are not merely difficult, but gut wrenching.

Our success had a great impact on our financial performance and market position; we did more business and made more money, and while people did in fact lose their jobs, we were fair to them and helped them with outplacement tools, industry contacts, and in some cases, educational opportunities. We managed the downsizing—just because the people were losing their jobs, that didn't absolve us from managing them to the best possible outcome for them. Why? That is what being a manager is all about—managing your resources to achieve an outcome that you define. In this case, I told my parental manager that she was in charge of what would happen to her people, and her parental weakness became a strength overnight once the decision was made.

In the absence of vision, an ill-defined vision, or even a great vision not communicated, you see the same thing: People working at a lethargic pace mixed in with people working at a frenzied pace—no progress and no distinction of achievement other than hallway conversations about who is working and who is not. Generally, everyone gets paid the same, increases are "peanut-butter spread," and if recognition exists, it is personality-based instead of accomplishment-based.

That is the importance of vision: It defines the environment in which you and your team will work; it defines the way you will approach your job every day; it defines your intensity, your timelines, your energy, and ultimately your success.

Vision defines the environment in which you and your team will work.

So, the question is, what is your vision?

Your Mission Statement

Out of a vision come questions about how you will achieve your vision—what companies commonly refer to as their *mission statement*, or their *mission*. A mission statement answers the question of how you will achieve your vision. For example, if your vision is to be among the top three players in your industry, your mission

A mission statement answers the question of how you will achieve your vision.

statement addresses the question of how. A mission statement leads with the answer: "To become the most effective sales force in delivering timely and effective products that lead the industry in creativity and low cost." That is how you will be one of the top players in the industry. It is your mission.

When our vision was to create value for shareholders, our mission was to become the best provider of financial services in our space, across financial, customer service, and compliance measurements. If we did that, then we would be profitable and sought after in the marketplace by customers, and that combination created value.

Don't get confused about a mission statement: It isn't the strategy or the plan or even the budget; it is simply the answer to the question of how will you accomplish the vision. It is the next logical level of communicating to a company about what the end game is. It makes the vision tangible, recognizable in the workplace, and another step closer for people to understand and ultimately join in, develop, and partake in the ownership of the vision.

It doesn't matter whether you are the CEO or the mailroom supervisor; you need to have a vision, and you need to have a mission that will carry out that vision. Otherwise, you will never get there; as a manager, you will never achieve the goals because you will never be able to get everyone focused at the same time on achieving success and, more importantly, recognizing success.

To successfully accomplish your vision, you need a clear mission to carry it out.

You might conclude that every sports team's vision is to win the championship, but some do it with defense and others with offense. Still others are very balanced, some are aggressive, and some are conservative. These styles are the mission. Remember, the mission answers the question of how. In 1985–86, the Chicago Bears were all about defense in attaining their goal of winning the Super Bowl, whereas the St. Louis Rams in 1999–2000 were the "greatest show on turf," denoting their offensive-minded approach.

These were two very different approaches to missions that would attain the exact same vision. The key to the mission statement is defining the things that will matter and then beginning to build them and perfect them in a manner that will achieve the vision.

Saying you want to be profitable is one thing, actually taking the steps to be profitable is quite another. When I was the chief financial officer at a large financial services institution, our division was not doing very well from a profit-and-loss measurement. When we began to focus on profitability, it became clear that the revenue generation, the margins, and the economics of our business simply could not support the expense base that had accumulated over the years. In good times we were profitable but had not focused on profitability. So we felt great that the division made $100 million—there were banners, paperweights, T-shirts, and slogans recognizing the $100 million accomplishment. What we didn't realize was that although we were a great $100 million division, we were probably a terrible $200 million division and just didn't see it because our mission at the time wasn't about profitability, it was about market share, and we were doing pretty well there, too.

> The key to the mission statement is to define the elements that matter and then build them and perfect them in such a way that will achieve the vision.

There is nothing wrong with making $100 million and leading in market share—unless, of course, your goal is profitability. When the market turned, we indeed realized we needed to change; the external factors forced us to change our mission, but interestingly, the vision of being the industry leader never changed. What changed was what that vision meant—how we became the leader changed for us. We now wanted to be the most profitable.

We needed to redefine the mission and adapt our activities and execution to reflect the mission. We succeeded, but it was a very difficult period for everyone to go through, mainly because we had not tooled the organization to be profit-conscious.

We made money; that wasn't the issue. The issue was we needed to make more, and frankly, that meant focusing on spending. Expense management is always a challenge. We will discuss that in a later chapter, but the point for this moment is that a mission statement should tell you how you will realize the vision. There are many ways to realize your vision—whichever one you pick will become your mission. Once you've chosen your mission, you must develop it (see Figure 1.1).

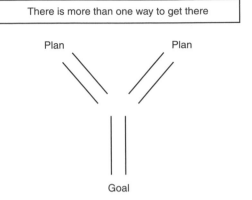

Figure 1.1
There is more than one way to reach your vision.

There is more than one way to get there

Plan   Plan

Goal

Developing Your Mission Statement

You develop a mission by first understanding what is happening in the market.

A mission is developed by beginning with market data and understanding what is happening in the market. You study the market and understand what market opportunities you can avail yourself of. Now, you may be thinking, "I am a mailroom supervisor; what possible market research do I need to do?" Well, here are a few thoughts for you. What will the demand on your mailroom be like next year, based on the company's plan? What are the trends in your industry in mailroom handling? What are other companies in your industry doing with their mailrooms? Bring in a few vendors (it's free) and ask them what they can do for you. What is the benchmark of number of employees to mail delivered that an outsourcer would use to provide the service? How do you compare to them? Why are you better? Why are you worse? And that is just the mailroom!

Managing isn't just for a particular department, unit, or level, and visions, mission statements, and missions themselves are not for some managers; they are for every manager.

Doing Market Research

Market research begins the mission and defines the path.

Market research begins the mission; it defines the path. Don't try to fit your capability into an opportunity; rather, look simply at the opportunity. You have heard the infamous statement that if the railroad industry thought of themselves as in the transportation business, they would have expanded into the airline industry and perhaps been able to continue successfully. Instead, they thought to themselves, "We are in the railroad industry"—a self-fulfilled doom.

Take a broad view of your market and understand what the opportunities will be in the next cycle. Understand what the characteristics of successful markets will be like and what a company would have to do to succeed in that market.

Market sources range from industry experts, to vendors, to customer research, to regulator views, to economic influences. All these are market factors, and you should develop a view on each one. A view is a position on the market—what do you think will happen as a result of those factors, and why? That becomes your market outlook.

You must understand what the characteristics of successful markets are and what a company has to do to succeed in that market.

You now have a vision, a mission, and a market outlook. So, suppose you run the accounting department—what does a market outlook look like, exactly? Will there be new accounting rules impacting your industry? What do the people you serve want from your department: more analytics, improved timing of results, streamlined expense recording processes? No matter what your department, you have a market—it is the people you serve, as well as your discipline as it relates to external factors. All of that will translate into the opportunity you have to avail yourself of in developing your mission.

Understanding the Competition

The final component in the market opportunity is the competition. What is the competition doing, and how do you compare to it? An analysis commonly referred to as a *SWOT analysis* is helpful in viewing the competition (see Figure 1.2). Strengths, weaknesses, opportunities, and threats are quantified in such an analysis, as if you were the competitor assessing yourself. This is particularly helpful in getting your sales force and marketing teams engaged in the market by forcing them to understand the competition from the inside out. Its byproduct is knowing the competition well enough to beat them.

A SWOT (strengths, weaknesses, opportunities, and threats) analysis is helpful in assessing the competition.

S trengths

W eaknesses

O pportunities

T hreats

Figure 1.2
SWOT analysis.

15

Competition, by the way, isn't limited to the sales and marketing teams. The human resources team, the legal team, the finance team, the treasury team—any department must best the comparable department in the competition's organization for the entire team to win strongly.

Every department must best the comparable department in the competition's organization for the entire team to win strongly.

A few years ago, there was a program in the financial services industry that, frankly, many of us thought was not legal, yet one competitor had figured it out. As with most regulations, the intent is always for a positive consumer experience. However, the government tends to, well, be the government, and the interpretations of the regulations actually had a negative impact on the industry. One competitor figured out the detail of the letter of the law and correctly interpreted it to be the advantage it was meant to be, and a new product was born.

It wasn't born of the marketing department, it wasn't the creative ideation sessions of a consultant working with the sales force—it was the legal department. The lawyers themselves understood that they were part of the competition, part of the game, and had something to offer. That mentality is as rare as it is crucial.

You have done a complete market scan, you have views on the opportunities, and you have a vision. Now for the mission—or if you had a mission going in, pause and validate it. Adjust it if you need to, but finalize it.

Vision, mission, and market outlook in hand, you now are ready to tackle the most difficult and most important part of defining yourself as a manager—your values (see Figure 1.3).

Figure 1.3
Vision, mission, and values: necessary components in management.

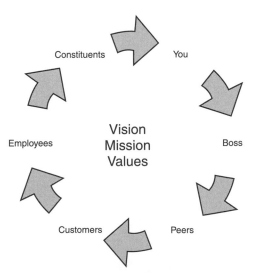

Your Values

The importance of values is often overlooked. Many times it is thought of as the softer side of managing, and therefore, in a managerial science developed by machismo creatures, it is frankly seen as B.S. The reality is that you will never have a greater tool to achieve success as a manager than the value system you and your employees choose to adopt. Why? Simple: Values guide people's actions. Particularly when process or technology isn't enough in a situation (and it seldom is), values will determine the outcome.

> When process or technology isn't enough in a situation, values will determine the outcome.

Values form a common bond in an organization, and although I am not a fan of thinking about an organization as a "family," I do believe that a family and an organization share the impact values have on each in that values form bonds. In business, bonds form teamwork, they fuel respect, and they dictate pace and often—very often—success.

The creation of a value system in an organization must be tied to the vision of the organization. For example, if your vision is to become the premier service provider in your industry, and your market research indicates that consumers want and value job knowledge, then one of your core values may in fact be knowledge. What exactly does that mean? Well, like any value that you may live by in your personal life, valuing a characteristic in the corporate or business world means that you are dedicated to that value, and that it means more to you than other attributes, which is why you will invest in it, nurture it, pursue it, reward it, and reinforce it. You will look for people in your organization who have knowledge, and they will stand out as successful. You will recruit people who have knowledge as a core threshold for hiring. You will reward people monetarily and non-monetarily who demonstrate knowledge.

> The value system must be tied to the vision of the organization.

In an environment where knowledge is a core value, you probably won't see entry-level jobs that require no experience. You won't see many administrative managers; you will see good managers who may be good administrators, but they will always have deep technical knowledge and may not always have good administrative capability. It depends on the remainder of the value system as to the makeup of the people. That is the importance of a value system; it defines the character of the organization.

Here again, much like the vision and mission, you must manage to the values, and that provides the connection of these three critical components of a manager's success. Values are far-reaching, and when practiced well, they are deeply rooted and become a common language and behavior of any organization.

Common organizational values that support your vision will be a crucial managerial tool.

When I was the COO of a midsized mortgage bank in the '90s, one of our core values was honesty. Seems pretty simple, doesn't it? What does honesty in the workplace mean to you? If you are like most people, it probably means not to lie or steal, and to tell the truth. Now, if those were the only attributes of an honest person, we would have a lot more of them than we do!

A value such as honesty starts with being honest with yourself, and that may mean a host of behaviors that need to be considered before one adopts honesty as a core value. Remember, a core value is simply a value that you will call out as what your team will live by; it isn't a license for or against any other value. So if honesty isn't a core value, that doesn't mean people are dishonest or that dishonesty is accepted.

A core value is a primary characteristic that supports the vision and will be looked for and emphasized in the organization.

A manager who desires honesty as a core value encourages people to raise their hand when they don't understand, encourages debate and disagreement as a means of perfecting an outcome, doesn't seek out those with a different opinion in a retaliatory manner, and emphasizes an environment of openness. Remember, openness also means standing up and saying things are going well when they are. We tend to think of things in a negative context when discussing management in the workplace, and that is neither healthy nor a good way to manage.

As we discuss honesty as a value, you can see how values will need to come together and interplay in the workplace. Honesty and teamwork are an interesting and misunderstood combination. People have said to me in focus groups, "I would have said something about that flawed process, but I wanted to be a good team player, and my team worked hard on that process." What? Being honest becomes a requirement of good teamwork when the two are in play at once. Core values become dependencies, not trade-offs, and that is an extremely important and difficult lesson that each team must learn out of the gate.

I had a customer service rep once who was on the phone with our customer and misplaced the customer's application for a credit card. This, of course, was back in the day of paper applications—

imagine that! The customer service rep said, "Sir, I lost your application paperwork." You can imagine the response—the customer immediately asked to speak to the president of the company. He was infuriated that his financial and personal information was "lost" and concerned that it would be found by the wrong person and his personal wealth and privacy were in jeopardy. In a panicked state, the rep transferred the call to my office.

I took the call, acknowledged the severity of the problem, and committed to an immediate callback within 20 minutes with an update and/or solution to the problem. It just so happened that the call center was in the same building I was in, and I felt like I might want to handle this one on a more personal basis, so I walked over to the call center and found the customer service rep. As I approached him, he stood up and said, "Hi, Mr. Meola. I know why you are here, and don't worry—I have found the file." He held up the file over his head with one hand, as if it were a trophy of some kind.

"Wow, that great," I said. "Where was it?"

"Well," he replied, "I had misfiled it here in the work queue." You see back in the old days, before we had imaging and workflow, we did it all with Pendaflex files. (I'll let you look that one up.)

Now it was time for engagement. As a manager, I always want to know what drives behavior, so I asked, "Why did you tell him it was lost?" He looked at me perplexed, almost as if to say, "Was there something else I could have said?" Then, shifting his eyes as people often do when they search for a response, he said, "Well, I couldn't lie to him. We are supposed to be honest!"

Ah, the core value kicks in! I looked at him and said, "It wasn't lost, though, so I guess you lied after all." We called the customer together and straightened out the mess, and everything was back on track.

The situation obviously called for a little debrief beyond the exchange, so I asked the customer service rep to stop in with his supervisor before he left. I assured him he wasn't in any kind of trouble—in fact, I said the visit was more for me to learn than it was for him. When he came by, much to my amazement he had figured out where he went wrong in his mind. "I leapt to a conclusion—that we lost the file—because we keep misfiling these applications with this new first-in-first-out method versus the old

Core values won't fail you if you truly understand them and apply them in the manner in which they were intended.

way of filing by application date, so I just assumed we lost it. I should have said, 'Let me gather the information I need and call you back to discuss your application'—that was the real truth of the situation."

Interesting lesson in core values here: They won't fail you if you truly understand them and apply them in the manner in which they were intended in the first place.

Selecting Core Values

There are many ways to determine core values—surveys that place point values on different values, internal focus groups to ascertain what people feel is important to accomplish the vision or mission, management discussion groups, or a combination of all of the above. Sometimes, in the interest of time, you may put three or four values out there that you believe are truly critical to the vision, and as long as you are open to being wrong on that assumption, you can begin to validate, morph, and mold into what will ultimately be the correct values for what you are trying to accomplish.

You must commit to and live by the core values you define.

Once you define the values, you must commit to them and truly live by them. Just like your personal values, they will be tested, and also just like your personal values, you will not always pass the test, but you must be committed to correcting course to maintain the value system every time there is a breach.

In some cases that corrective action may be extreme, and it may even challenge the values, the vision, and your success in a manner you did not foresee, but I caution you to remain true to your values.

In an organization where we had a phenomenal performer—there is simply no other way to describe this salesperson's performance—a situation arose in which the individual violated a core value in a very clear, deliberate, and public way. He was the top-producing salesperson in the area and had singlehandedly made the market for us. We knew terminating this individual would cause a threat to us in the market because he would immediately go to our top competitor. We also knew that because he was an outstanding performer in his area, he was looked upon as a role model, and we knew that this was a threshold moment for the value system we had created.

But it really was an easy decision to make if we made it by our core values—if our values meant something more than the paper they were written on, and if they were truly tied to the vision of who we were to become. We terminated the salesperson. And in fact, he went to the competitor, and they gained market share in that market from us as a result.

I can tell you, however, that as a result of that one decision, the organization came together throughout the country in a way that it never would have otherwise. People began to embrace the changes we were making and believe in the vision, mission, and values that we were managing by. And yes, we were successful, and eventually we were successful in that market again—only this time it was consistent with our vision, and as a result, it was sustainable beyond any one person.

It is this commitment to a vision, guided by unwavering values each step of the way, that creates success and, more importantly, sustains it. I can't tell you how many organizations I have entered where if they had just adhered to what I read on their walls and on the paperweights on their desks, they would not have needed a turnaround or overhaul. It's no wonder that we see so many times the answer is to get back to basics. The basics are vision and values.

I will tell you, it took two-and-a-half years to rebuild the market we lost in my company after letting go of that salesperson, but we built it the right way. My senior management thought I was nuts to fire our top salesperson, but they supported me, and that is why it is key to shop your vision, mission, and values with your senior management and get their buy-in and support outside of the testing time!

Syncing Your Values

Once you determine your values, just like with your vision, you need to make sure you are in sync with the company and with your management. Then you need to share both over and over again, endlessly. As new people come into and out of your area of responsibility, you will need to ensure that values and vision are understood by all. Remember, the more you talk about it, the more you will bring it about. The more people who understand the vision, values, and mission, the more talent can be utilized to bring it about.

> Just like your personal values, your core values will be tested. You must be committed to maintaining the value system every time there is a breach.

> Commitment to a vision, guided by unwavering values each step of the way, creates and sustains success.

> You need to make sure you are in sync with the company and with your management.

I cannot overemphasize that vision, mission, and values are critical for any manager, regardless of the size of the department. These aren't only reserved for CEOs or a large-scale company.

My first manager job was in an accounts payable department that was dedicated to the distribution aspects of an oil company. I will never forget when I got the initial call that I was going to be promoted to manager of that department. The department was considered the worst accounting unit in the company. Every month you would hear stories about how they screwed up the monthly closing process, caused other areas to work overtime because of their errors—they were regarded as a group of misfits. No one—and I do mean *no one*—wanted to be moved into that department.

Vision, mission, and values are critical for any manager, regardless of the size of the department.

So, when I got the call into the controller's office and he told me they had made the decision to make me the manager, I asked him what I had done wrong to deserve such a fate. He laughed and he said to me that he thought I had great leadership qualities, a passion for people, and was very well thought-out in the things I did. He told me that this job would define my career—if I turned this department into a respectable unit, I would be known as a "problem solver." And problem solvers have great futures!

It was a great sell, and frankly, I had no choice but to buy. I asked him the question I heard so often asked in big meetings: "If you had a magic wand and could wave it over this department, what would happen?" He smiled, and later I would find out that the smile I saw on his face was brought about by the fact that with my question, I had confirmed his decision to put me in that area. Also, as he would tell me later, it confirmed in his mind that I would be successful.

He said, "Tony, I want this department to be the best accounting in finance team in the company—period."

Well, I had asked, so there it was. I was to manage a department that was widely known for its incompetence, had its personnel referred to as misfits, and was the department no one wanted to join. That's the group I was supposed to make the best unit in the company!

I had the weekend to think about what to do. Over that weekend, I began my management career. I didn't know it at the time, but most of what you are reading now was born that weekend. It was the beginning of becoming a student, teacher, and mentor all at once. The one piece of advice that I learned that weekend was a piece I now will share with you.

As a young accountant in the late '70s, part of my job was to submit my journal entries to the keypunch department, who would then convert them to punch cards. They would call me, and I would pick the punch cards up and submit them to the electronic data processing department for entry into the computer. (Okay, you can stop laughing now.) The advice that changed my career and helped me that weekend came one day from our CFO.

The deadline for that keypunch unit submission was 4:00 p.m. I had quite a few entries to make that day, and I got through them all and raced down three flights of stairs to deliver them. I greeted the keypunch supervisor as I always did and put the papers on the table. And I could not believe his response, which was, "Sorry Tony, it's 4:05. I can't accept them." I was shocked, angered, frustrated, and bewildered all at once. After a brief exchange that wasn't very pleasant, I walked away, journal entries in hand.

As I approached the stairwell, I saw our CFO waiting for the elevator. He noticed the look on my face and said, "Hey Tony, how's it going?" I thought, "Here is a chance to tell this guy how stupidly the place runs," so I responded with, "It would be a lot better if people weren't so narrow-minded." I proceeded to tell him the events of the past 30 minutes, colored somewhat to favor my position, of course. He asked me if I had a few minutes to go to his office. I thought to myself, "What an opportunity this is—a six-level jump up to the top to talk to the big guy himself." This was a major career opportunity, I thought. I did not know how right I was, but I also had no idea of the advice I was about to receive.

"So, what's the issue here, Tony?" was his lead question with a get-to-the-point tone.

"Well, these guys in keypunch wouldn't keypunch the journal entries because I was five minutes late. They have no idea how important these are to close the books or the amount of work they now have created for five minutes—it's unbelievable!" I paused, having made the point emphatically.

I wasn't at all ready for his response. "Tony, what do you want to do in your career?" I was a bit stunned; I usually always try to out-think the opponent, but I was clueless on where he was heading.

"I want to be CFO—your job," I said, figuring that was a good start.

"Well," he said, "then you need to think like a CFO starting now. While I agree with you from an accountant's view, think about your situation as if you were the CFO. If every department is five minutes late, then what does that do to the closing schedule of the company? And if they make that exception to the rule for you, who else do they make it for? Is it five minutes or ten, maybe eleven? How do you control it?"

I felt myself sink back in the chair a bit as he continued. "So, what do you want to change? I expect your keypunch manager had the same things to say about you for being late that you did about him for not understanding the importance of your work. I might conclude you didn't understand the importance of your work if you let it get to the point of a missed deadline, but this isn't about these journal entries—this is about how you think about things. It's too late to begin your career as a CFO when you get there, my friend—start now!"

It is that advice to think like the role you want to play in life that will allow you to see and hear things you never would otherwise and that will allow you to be successful. Your role as a manager is never too small to use these management practices and principles, and to master them is to fulfill your objective as a manager.

> Your role as a manager is never too small to use management practices and principles.

That weekend, I sat and said, "My going-in position is to become the best accounting department there, the one everyone envies, wants to be part of, and wants to emulate. I want it to be recognized by everyone who encounters it as the standard of excellence."

When I showed up Monday, I went to my office—a fishbowl setup—and stayed in there for about a half hour, making some notes and watching the people come in. You could see by the looks on their faces that they were concerned, even fearful of the young manager with the reputation for getting things done and working endless hours. The manager, the word on the street had it, that was hand-selected by the CFO and management to do this job.

I called them all in my office—it barely fit 22 of them, all clericals and two assistant supervisors. I introduced myself and said that I was excited to be there and was looking forward to the role and the success that we would have as a department.

I said, "My goal for us is to be the best accounting department in this organization—no matter how you measure it, we will be the best." I further told them I wanted to meet with each one of them for an hour the first week to get their ideas and views, and that we would form a plan to be the best.

As the meeting ended, one of the assistant supervisors stayed behind. He swung the door shut and said to me, "That was the same speech the last three guys in two years have given us. Let me tell you something—this place sucks. This is an accounts payable department, and you are always going to fail at something—vendors, reporting, timely bill pay—it's just too much, and no one has a clue how screwed up this place really is."

It was the first test of the vision, 90 seconds after I laid it out. Frankly, it angered me, and I said to him, "So quit—but don't come in here tomorrow. If that's what you truly believe, I can't use you here." I didn't look at him; I just dropped my head to some paperwork, and he stood there stunned and then slowly left.

I thought I gave the speech of my life; I thought I rallied the troops and we were on our way to the top, and that guy gave me a dose of reality and taught me a vision is only that—a vision. I have learned now that it is essential to have a vision, but I have also learned you have to have something much more than a vision to succeed: You have to have a relentless commitment to it before you begin, because it will be challenged, it will struggle, and it will take conviction and perseverance for you to execute it.

I sat in my office and suddenly realized that I had committed 22 hours in this week to one-on-ones, and it would be Tuesday before I could even start! Remember, give yourself time: Creating a vision, a mission, and your values will take 60 to 90 days. I know that now; I only wish I knew it then.

You have to have more than a vision to succeed: You have to have a relentless commitment to it before you begin.

My first meeting was with a clerical employee who had been with the company for 20 years. She remembered the days when the department worked well, and she began to tell me how the "young people" had ruined it—by the way, I was 28 years old! The next clerical worker told me how she got confused between all the different-colored keypunch pads—white for thirty days net, red for transportation, green for dry freight, and so on. She said in the old days there was one color and it was much easier.

Then the younger crowd came in, and they complained about the older people—their slow pace, that they never handed off the work on schedule to them for processing, that they always had to tell a long story when they handed the younger people the work. Then their supervisor—always talks to them and walks around doing nothing all day, then freaks out when everything is due. They were all honest, they all had a point of view, and they all hated the place.

I was overwhelmed, but the process had served me well. Because I had scheduled these 22 hours in 4 days, I had no time to react. I was gathering all the data points, and although I didn't realize it, the accelerated schedule forced me to be patient, not overreact, and not manage from the floor. When you hold focus groups to discuss the vision, what your goals are, and what the challenges will be, that isn't where you solve the problems—that is where you gather the data points and where you reflect on them until the solutions begin to gel.

The problem here was more than attitude—it was the environment that created the attitude. People had issues and problems and they complained about them, but no attempt was made to fix them. We were a department that processed high volumes of paperwork, and the output was specially designed. A formula for disaster. They tried to put the output into the process: Special categories, specific info, even the sorting of reports was all managed by the input process. The setup was all wrong; we had mass processing for specialized output.

Then came my talk with the assistant supervisor. He came in and said, "I have watched you here for the last three days, talking to everybody and writing stuff down. Do you really think you can fix this place—I mean, *really*?" I said that I thought I could, but we needed a plan. It was pretty screwed up, that was for sure, but I thought we could fix it—I really did. He asked me if I wanted him to stay. I was honest with him—I told him not if he didn't believe it could be fixed. He told me he needed the job but he didn't see how we could. But, he was willing to try whatever we came up with.

I told him he had 90 days, and we would revisit it. This is a methodology I have used for 30 years—I give people 90 days before I judge them, and I owe that principle to him. Sometimes I know on Day 1 and spend 89 days validating my theory; other times I don't know until Day 89, but I always know by 90 days—always.

Again, don't rush yourself. On Day 3 I got my first phone call from my boss, and he asked me how it was going. I said okay, which concerned him a bit (versus great!), and I told him it would take me a week before I had a plan for him to discuss. A week—what a mistake that was. You can't diagnose a department and its interactions internally and externally, get a read on its talent, and understand the process fixes you'll need until you see it perform through three life cycles at a minimum, but I was 28, and a week was all I thought I needed!

After 22 hours of conversations, I charted out the data I had collected into like statements and issues. So the vision was clear in my mind, at least, and I had communicated to all the staff and heard from each one why that vision wouldn't work—and frankly, how great it would be if it could work.

Vision in hand: To be the best accounting department in the company by any measure. But now what was the mission? Remember, the mission is the set of activities that will allow you to reach the vision. So in this case, I had to understand the external definition to which we would be held to be the best.

I first met with the manager of what was regarded as the best accounting department in the company. Supply and distribution accounting was the most highly regarded department in the company; they had a track record of the most promotions and on-time closing schedule, and they were considered the best. Honestly, when I met with him and told him I wanted my unit to be the best, he laughed out loud.

"Tony, what makes us the best is we are good—period! Each guy out there is the best at what he does, and I make sure he is every day. I review their work, I monitor their performance to goal, I take action when they miss deadlines, and my deadlines are always ahead of any corporate deadline. The people that use our information never have to question it; they know it's good because it comes from us."

Develop trust through expertise.

He then said he used a report writer to format information in any manner the user wanted it. Given the dilemma I faced, where we created work in the department to make sure the reporting output came out the way users could use it, I asked about it. He said there were only two guys in the company who knew the programming for it—back in 1978, not many people were embracing user-driven programming.

Use technology to deliver information.

When I saw my friends in keypunch, they told me my group was never on time and often missed the detail journal cutoff, which caused topside entries with no detail for management to see or draw information from. This was interesting because it was a direct tie to my department's complaint that the supervisor would walk around all day and then go crazy at the last minute to get work done.

Then I spoke to the area we serviced—ironically, I couldn't get on the manager's schedule there, so I offered a Saturday or Sunday meeting. He was so taken aback that I offered those days that he called me directly, which was unheard of—a senior VP placing a call to an accounting manager! He saw me right away; he saw the relentless commitment I had and later told me that the invite and subsequent conversation told him that I would rise in the company and he could build upon my success in his own area—something he would share with me three years later.

His point was clear: He wanted information in certain formats, and it was his idea to color-code everything in our department and have all special classes of delivery and keypunch rules and so on that required too much specialization at the point of entry by people who simply would never be able to master the rules he seemingly thought of daily.

At this point I was ready to approach the mission statement. The issue was that my department was in the information business, but they didn't have a clue. They thought they were an accounts payable group. Remember the supervisor's comment that "we are just an accounts payable department?" Well, we weren't—that was the issue.

And so I created a mission statement: To create information through the use of technology and expertise in a timely manner that would enable all of our consituents to better perform their jobs.

Now it was time to work on the values, except that back then I didn't know they were our values. I didn't know that managers create and manage an environment where people can excel or fail. Instead, I positioned these as the nonnegotiables:

- We work as a team.
- We embrace technology.
- We manage to timeliness.
- We think like a user of our information.

That was it, pure and simple.

So, there you have it—a vision, mission, and values of a 23-person department. I imagine you are wondering how it turned out. Well, I am writing a book on management, so that should be a clue! Within two years we were recognized as the best accounting department in the company. I eventually became the manager of the supply and distribution accounting department, and later the controller over both areas in addition to a few other departments.

Some highlights of that run: I took my assistant supervisor out of being an assistant supervisor and trained him on the programming language, with the commitment that it would be his contribution to the department to deliver reporting information the way users wanted it. I then streamlined those journal entries into three colors and assigned each person one color. (Remember the good-old-days conversation I had with the 20-year clerical worker?) Additionally, I eliminated as many handoffs as I could. I created functional experts that dealt with the same payment type and vendors so they could develop their expertise. (Remember my conversation with the supervisor of the other accounting group? My people were now experts.)

I also reworked our work schedule to eliminate a day from the closing schedule, meeting with all our external managers and departments and changing their deadlines of information to me, with the promise of better reporting and eliminating their downstream rework of our information. That also took the pressure off the closing deadlines for my team: We had a cushion—one we seldom used, but when we did need it, it was always there.

I expanded the technology training over time to our younger clericals, who seemed very interested in it. We turned out reports in formats never done before, and in our second year, we began a database project that managed our trucking invoices and internal maintenance.

Suddenly, we were producing information that made a difference, our people had exciting jobs, and I let them know of our accomplishments every month. I posted on my board the timeliness statistics of our journal entries by person and our department timeliness of reporting and handoffs. Month after month, it was 100 percent. People wanted to work for us because not only were we good, but I added something that the supply and distribution accounting department never had—FUN! We celebrated when we submitted our last journal entry on time, we had pizza when we worked late, we laughed at some of our crazy times, I recognized employees each month individually at department meetings, and we talked about being the best. We talked about the vision.

There were issues, and we used our values to resolve them. Timeliness was important, so we would help each other out through teamwork to ensure the department was timely. Issues arose that made us adopt or see clearly a value: A nonnegotiable we didn't have was accountability—I fired three people because they did not give the effort to timeliness and were constantly needing to be bailed out.

People understood my commitment to the vision, mission, and values, and they enjoyed success—never underestimate how much people enjoy success. The age thing disappeared, and the attitudes improved. Why? Because we had a vision, we had a reason to come to work in the morning. We were on a mission, and we could see the progress because we looked, we measured, and we were accountable to each other and to ourselves.

We rallied around our assistant supervisor to help him keypunch his programs, we designed reports at the request of our constituents, and we kept shortening that schedule. We were closed two days before everyone else in the company most months, and we had it down to a science by the beginning of our third year.

People from my group came to me daily with ideas for how to do things differently, better, and faster. They didn't get paid more for it, but I recognized them. I named reports and processes after them and asked my manager to come down and shake their hand. Every week we had a staff meeting where I explained how we were doing, brutally honestly—if we were bad, I would say it, but I would always ask why we weren't performing. Sometimes they responded in silence; other times they would tell me the issues.

I also learned something interesting: When we were at our peak performance, if we were five minutes late to keypunch, they accepted it! Yes, you read that right—they accepted it because we were always on time, and if there was a need for another group to step up to support us they would, because we were always there for them, month after month!

Vision, mission, and values are for every department manager. Understanding the obstacles in the way, defining from others' views what success looks like and communicating it to your people, and holding them to a standard of excellence in execution and behavior—that's what it is all about.

Whether you are a CEO, a director, a manager, a supervisor, or an assistant supervisor, two people or two hundred or two thousand, it honestly doesn't matter. You need a vision, you need a mission, and you need to be in touch with your values. The more the creation of these comes from those who need to execute them, the better the understanding, the stronger the success, and the greater the accomplishment that awaits you.

Understand the obstacles, define together what success looks like, and hold your people to a standard of excellence in execution and behavior.

To become the best manager you can be over the next 90 days, begin the process to formulate you vision, mission, and values now!

Chapter 2

The Management System

- Assessing Your Team
- Establishing Initial Objectives
- Having a Plan
- Managing Horizontally
- Navigating Obstacles

There have been many books, articles, and essays revolving around the "first 90 days," and for the most part I have read them all. But what is missing from all of them is the results orientation that is really the essence of a 90-day plan. The true objective of any management action plan is to allow you to learn how best to deal with your department to achieve success and to provide you with different levels of interaction with your people so you get to know their strengths and weaknesses. You then need to make an assessment as to whether this is a team with which you can go on the mission to achieve your vision.

Assessing Your Team

You are going to spend a lot of time with this team, and they will be an important part of your success. I once worked for a manager who told me, "Tony, your team feeds your family." Interesting thought, but also very true in many ways. The correct match and selection of your team can help you overcome more obstacles than any other part of management.

Correctly matching and choosing your team will help you overcome many obstacles in your management role.

You see this in major sports teams, particularly where there is a drafting process, such as in the NBA or the NFL, where there is such a noticeable and published selection. What do you usually find? For one thing, it's usually not the most talented person or a particular position that is the correct choice—what is more common to their success is their fit into the existing team, how they play the game, and their chemistry in fitting the situation the team is faced with. If you haven't recognized it, I will make it clear: It's their values, pure and simple—how their values fit in with the team or what you are aiming for, particularly in the case of change.

In a management case, most of the time the team exists when you get there, so the approach you need to take is more of an assessment than a build, but be clear that it is both. Whether or not you realize it, you will hire every one of them into your team either explicitly or implicitly, but whatever you do, please do not hire them by default. When I take over an organization, I give everyone a page in my notebook and I collect my observations on them. Then, after 90 days, I either hire them or I don't. Sometimes they leave sooner, but I never hire them sooner. After all, they are going to feed my family!

I once took over an organization that was rather large—3,000-plus people—and it was divided into three main areas, all reporting to one person. When I showed up, I brought a division with me that had about 2,000 people itself. During our first discussion, my new direct report and I spoke about the business, the state of the industry, and the current challenges and successes. We talked about philosophies and how we approach things; we also talked about personal careers and shared stories and people we had in common. At the end of the discussion, he looked at me and asked, "Did I pass the test?" I said I wasn't administering one, and he pressed further. "Look, I have a family, I need a job and a career, and I am a big boy, so tell me: Am I in or out?"

In a management case, the team usually exists when you get there, so the approach you need to take is more of an assessment than a build—but be clear that it is both.

Honestly, if I had a good read at that point that the guy wouldn't be on my team, I probably would have said something stupid, because in that situation, when you've made up your mind and it is your decision, the only thing to do is to be honest. You can always work out the exit, but you really owe it to people to be honest. I truly believe that, and I try to live by it.

Unfortunately, in this case I really didn't know whether he could be a player on my team because although he said all the right things, I wasn't sure how he would react to the changes ahead. So I told him, "You will be the guy who decides whether you stay on the team. I enjoyed our conversation, but I don't make a decision unless I need to make it, so if you are asking me to hire you right now, I am telling you I am not ready to do that. But if you are asking me if there is any reason for you to look for a new role, I would say no—you have a major role here. I need more than an hour to tell you whether you are my choice. That said, I like what you have said and even how you approached this question."

When he left my office, he encountered our human resources director by chance (or at least that was the story), and he said he didn't think I liked him and he wasn't sure it was going to work out.

So, what went wrong? The first 90 days is all about expectations, and that is what every management book and course misses. It's about setting the expectations for the 90-day period, not solving the world's problems in 90 days.

The first 90 days is all about expectations.

If I could redo that conversation, I would have set the expectation before we began by saying, "Here is how I operate: I will take the next 90 days to develop our vision and mission and values with you and assess the talent we have to achieve that vision, and I'll let you know what changes I think we need to make to achieve it."

That is what I now do any time I take over an area, and I am true and unwavering to it. What went wrong in my discussion with that manager was that he was on an interview and I was not.

Any time there is a change—a new boss, a change in the way the existing boss is thinking about things, or an exercise aimed at betterment—it will create anxiety, and people don't do well with anxiety. A manager's role is always to alleviate anxiety by bringing clarity and direction so people can achieve their potential. It is that potential you are assessing in a nutshell—beyond, of course, their technical ability.

Establishing Initial Objectives

The first rule to being a better manager in 90 days is to let people know what to expect in those 90 days. The only way to do that is to lay out a schedule of what the first 90 days will look like, how you will run your area during that time, and what your objectives will be.

Lay out a schedule of what the first 90 days will look like, how you will run your area during that time, and what your objectives will be.

The objectives are always the same:

1. Understand the current state of the business.
2. Identify any immediate issues or improvements.
3. Begin the process of establishing the vision, mission, and values under which you will operate.
4. Ensure that you are organized for the task.
5. Assess the talent to get you there.

That's it. Anything more can't get done; anything less and you haven't done anything.

Understanding the Current State of the Business

Understanding the current state of the business isn't as easy as you may think. It involves a number of views through various lenses—senior management, colleagues, managers, employees, auditors, and constituents such as customers, regulators, or whomever the knowledge of performance assessment ultimately rests with. This is different than the vision or what it should be— this is what it is! You should have the same discussion with each constituent you meet with—cover where you are and where you want to be each time you sit down to discuss the department—but make certain you get both perspectives, the here and now and the future.

Discussion is a very limited and defined format. You also have reports that are published every day—hundreds of them pour out of a printer, an email box, or whatever your favorite medium is. You need to read them and comprehend what they tell you. But how do you know which ones matter?

Ask! Have each direct report give you the report or set of reports that he or she looks at daily, weekly, and monthly in that exact category with a brief write-up or headline as to what the report shares.

> Understanding the current state of the business involves considering a number of views through various lenses.

If there is an established reporting process already, such as a monthly report (outside of the normal review time), set up an all-day meeting to review in depth the last report published. Here you will gain knowledge of the report and knowledge of your direct report's presentation skills and interaction. Also, doing it collectively will be a team exercise, and you will see the team dynamic.

If you don't have a monthly business review, then you need to establish one. It should be once a month at minimum, because you need to review your mission in detail and make course corrections if you are to achieve your vision.

> Establish a monthly business review if one doesn't exist already.

Set aside time in your day to read the reports. It could be after work, before work, during work...but regardless of when it is, do set aside a time and read the reports. After reading each one, make a conscious assessment of whether your team is on course or off course. Ask yourself things like, "What questions do I have for clarity? What do I want to communicate that I like and what do I want to communicate that I don't?" Now you know why I believe in the "vital few" concept in reporting—because I really read them!

My direct reports write me a weekly email that summarizes their business for the week, advises me of what they think I should know, and asks any questions or seeks any input they need. I read and respond to those emails every weekend. Some people read the Sunday comics with coffee, but I have found reading my direct reports' emails more helpful to my success as a manager—and, at times, equally as entertaining!

You need to get your finger on the pulse of your current existence—by holding meetings, reviewing reports, and getting the views of multiple members of the organization.

In addition to holding specific meetings to understand what is working and what is not working, as well as beginning the process of reviewing the business in the form of reports, you will need to get the views of the members of the organization, from mid-line managers to employees. Depending on the size of the organization, this can take the form of focus groups, coffee with the boss, and so on. Nowadays, you can also use blogs, webmail, and all sorts of tools. It's all about getting your finger on the pulse of your current existence.

When given the assignment of taking on an 8,000-person organization, I realized that getting in touch with the people themselves would be a full-time job. So, I hired a firm that had a product that took a survey of the same five questions every day to get the pulse of the organization. Every Thursday, employees got to comment on, ask, or suggest anything they wanted to. The data was sorted by cost center and given to managers—it was anonymous. It was a virtual daily focus group of sorts, and it was a keen measurement of what we were trying to establish. On a scale of 1 to 7, with 1 being no and 7 being yes, we would ask:

1. Do you know what you need to perform at your best today?
2. Do you feel energized today?
3. Are you proud to work here?
4. Are you getting the help you need?
5. Will tomorrow be better?

We would read the comments on Thursdays. Our commitment to employees was that we would read the comments and, as a management team, act accordingly—nothing more nothing less. And frankly, we did—we devoted 20 minutes a week to the comments that were made on Thursdays. The sample analysis and trending that was in the program itself identified common words, key themes, and so on.

Understanding the current state of the business is one of the first goals of the next 90 days.

So, understanding the current state of the business is one of the first goals of the next 90 days—understanding it in such a way that you can write the current state of the business with the appropriate quantifiable measurements that define that state.

"We have no momentum" is an unquantifiable statement. When people surveyed scored a 3 on the question "Will tomorrow be better?" I quantified momentum!

The question you need to ask is how do you know? What is your standard of measurement? Then you can begin to measure it.

I worked in an area where people in a focus group told me they worked way too much overtime, and they did. Each person averaged about 15 hours a week of overtime and a half day on Saturday. When I asked why, there were as many reasons as people in the room and then some.

I asked to see the overtime reports for the organization and began to get them daily. When I saw larger numbers, I began to ask why. Mostly, it dealt with the fact that a system was down or unavailable. That led to discussions around my table about system performance, which led to an end-to-end analysis of our system up time or availability. It seems that the technology department, in an effort to keep costs down, was sharing servers, scheduling production times, and so on in a more high-risk manner to meet their budget. They *had* met their budget, by the way, but the rest of the place had an overtime issue.

When I asked managers whether there was a lot of overtime, their response was that it varied by department. But everyone had a capacity model and no one was too far off the staffing levels, so the headcount wasn't the issue. They had various productivity initiatives going to address overtime, but no one saw a common thread that the daily overtime reports painted until we began to review after that focus-group feedback.

Obtain a quantifiable understanding of the business, sourced by discussion, reports, reviews, and interaction, and write it down. Validate it with your direct reports and employees. This provides a common view of where you are. I like to call it the *starting line* or *baseline*—now you know where they are, and *they* know you know where they are!

> You need a baseline that provides a common view of where you are.

Identifying Immediate Issues

Next you need to begin to identify those things for which you can enable quick solutions or improvements and any urgent issues that may need your attention.

I recall getting a tour of a facility when I first took it over in the early '90s. It was a campus-type setting of three buildings. As we were walking from one building to the next, we saw a young man with a cart of reports going between buildings. About 15 minutes later, as we walked from Building 2 to Building 3, we saw the

It's important to identify those things for which you can enable quick solutions and any urgent issues that may need your attention.

same young man with the same cart and some different reports. Later in the day, same thing. These buildings weren't exactly close to each other, so I asked the manager showing me around, "What does that guy with the reports do with these carts?"

He told me that they only had one high-speed printer, and it was in the accounting department. So when people used the printer from other buildings, that guy's job was to deliver the reports. I asked how long he has been doing that for a living and about how much we paid him. To my surprise, he made about $18,000—maybe an entry-level clerical salary at the time—and he had been doing it for two years. I wondered how much time and productivity we lost waiting for him to deliver the cart of reports. I asked the manager to review the situation and let me know what was happening.

It turns out that the accounting department had moved about two years ago and took their high-speed printer with them, and 100 percent of the high-speed printing was now in Building 2. Of course, everyone hated the fact that they had to wait for any large report to be delivered, so they were buying their own printers to print out pieces of the reports they used—and yet they *still* printed the full report, just to have!

We reduced printed report lines by 65 percent in three months, our report runner became a mailroom employee with a career path, and we upgraded to smart printers across the place, matching the printer to the type of work. That was an example of a quick fix!

Other issues you will discover—backlogs, customer service issues, staffing, facilities, equipment, all environmental-type issues that slow any company down at times in the day-to-day workload—are examples of the things you need to identify. Concentrate on things that annoy people or kill them—the middle stuff takes too much time for the first 90 days.

Concentrate first on addressing the issues that really annoy people!

You can't solve all the issues, but go after them from either end of the spectrum. The one thing I would caution you about is that during this time, you should always bring everything back to your team—your direct reports—and ask them what they want to do about it.

Remember, you are assessing them at the same time as you are understanding the business, identifying issues, and establishing your organization's vision, mission, and values. Never fall into the trap of managing from the focus-group chair or from the floor. I call that *hero managing*—you are the boss; you don't need to prove yourself by decree. Bring the issues you discover to your team and let them articulate potential solutions. Your job is to bring the best solutions to the table and at times decide which one you want based on the direction you are trying to establish.

To get at the hidden issues of an organization, have your managers ask their staff for examples of things that could be quick hits for momentum. Ask managers for the two or three most critical issues.

Audit reports are a major key for any new manager to understand the issues in an organization. After reading the third report, pattern recognition sets in, and you will see the landscape in a unique way. Audit is a different view from the line—it is a view that, as a manager, you need access to. A review of all audit issues and reports is in order in the first two weeks of any manager's tenure.

Here is another opportunity to interact with and assess your team. You will see how they react to criticism, how they rationalize behaviors, how they take (or do not take) action, and most importantly, how they correct course.

I had a manager who had a failed audit prior to my taking over the area that he was a part of. When I called him to discuss the failed audit, he pointed out that the department was understaffed, they had training issues, and he had no support from the previous management to fix the issues.

I pointed out to him that he committed to a number of fixes in the audit and asked him about his progress. He was pretty vague but essentially said some things were done, others were in process, and still others were not begun. I asked whether he had a plan for when all the points would be addressed satisfactorily. His response was not a written one, but he did have a plan.

I suggested that he write down exactly, point by point, how he would fix the issues; let me know what we had to do to support it; and then review it all with me. I let him know that we would set up a biweekly meeting to track his progress.

This may not surprise you, but that manager quit about six weeks to the day later. The combination of quantifiable timelines, specific goals, and progress were not the way he managed, but they were what I value in management. His department fixed those

Never fall into the trap of hero managing. Let your team articulate potential solutions to issues.

Ask managers to share the two or three most critical issues that come up at their staff meetings.

You should review all audit issues and reports during the first two weeks of your tenure.

issues—yes, we had to add staff and do some process revisions, but we had a timetable communicated to people, everyone became part of the solution, and the plan was tracked on the department whiteboards with numbers and dates. The feeling of accomplishment quickly replaced the stigma of a failed audit.

Managing is always a simultaneous, omnipresent event.

In addition, a common practice and approach to audit findings was formed. The sharing of the plan and how to establish and track it promoted teamwork in the organization, and the success of the collective plans gave people a sense of momentum that we were getting somewhere—for a good reason, because we were!

I cannot overemphasize the fact that managing not only during the first 90 days, but always, is a simultaneous, omnipresent event. You are working on everything at once in everything you do, and that is how people will see you.

If you are handling an audit issue, a small issue, or a personal traction; responding to a public forum; or just walking in as a manager, you are making a statement.

After that manager left, people understood what the expectation of success looked liked, and after the unit accomplished its audit remediation plan, they had a model of it. A value came out of there as well—we learned that as an organization, we value teamwork and communication.

To achieve your vision, you must understand the current state of your business, identify key issues that negatively impact productivity, and address the issues with your team.

As a manager, you always need to understand your current state of business, identify key issues and those annoyances that drain productivity, and address the issues with your team in such a way that you can assess their abilities. That is how you perfect the organization and achieve your vision.

It seems like a lot and can be overwhelming to manage in this fashion unless you have a systematic approach to your management style—one that establishes feeding mechanisms for the information and processes you need to manage to succeed. This takes time to set up, but once you establish a system for managing in this fashion, you will never let it go.

Each manager is different—after all, managers are people, and people are certainly unique. But all of us have habits and schedules in our daily lives. You may be an early-morning exerciser who wakes up, runs a mile or two, and then hits the shower and sits down to a granola breakfast with your newspaper. Or maybe you run on the treadmill while watching CNN and grab a banana as you run out the door.

The point is that it doesn't matter as long as it works for you. Management style and systems are no different. They have one condition and one only—they need to work for you, and not you for them!

Your management system needs to work for you, not you for it!

By now I hope you know that your true north will be your vision and values. You will establish a mission to get there from here, and you know where "here" is because you understand the current state of the business.

Establishing an Organized Management System

You have read the audit reports, you know the issues you heard from people, and your team is working on many solutions to the quick hits and urgent matters. You understand the capabilities of those around you, and you are assessing and updating your thoughts on all of it. So now you need to put in a mechanism to sustain it all in a manner that is natural within a system. Just like the runner who has to run in the morning looks forward to it, the manager who has to manage will look forward to it if the system works for him.

A management system is all about repetition. People love repetition for one reason and one reason only—they know what to expect, and when they do, they can deliver and feel a sense of accomplishment.

Management systems are all about repetition.

Daily Meetings

At the cornerstone of running your department is information. You need a daily inflow of reports, and that information should be part of your morning meeting. Each morning you should bring your department or department heads together to review your reports, compare them to your expectations, and hear from them (and they from you) about the state of the department. If you are a floor supervisor, it's as simple as a huddle meeting. If you are a CEO it could be over coffee, but the objective in either case is to look at the daily metrics, see the performance, and talk about the day ahead.

You should have a daily meeting with your department or department heads to discuss the state of the department.

This strategy puts you on the same page as a unit and can address anything that needs to be addressed. More than that, it gives your team a common starting point and a place to go for discussion every 24 hours. Remember, you are assessing talent during this time, so the more you engage the points of input you have, the better you will make the decision about who is on your team.

Daily huddle meetings give your team a common starting point and a venue for discussion every 24 hours.

This isn't a staff meeting, it is a huddle meeting. It usually begins with a statement by the manager as to the business of the day. This should be followed by a lightning-round review of the key metrics, with simple statements such as, "We're on track," "No issues," "We have a problem here," "I need some IT support today," "The phones are out,"—whatever issues will hurt or help the performance. Trends emerge daily, and you can see them emerge right before your eyes, but more importantly, you can work them each day.

A second round around the table or on the phone would be any key updates. So the first round is management information key statistics, the second round is for key updates, and the third round is for questions. Then you are finished. My daily meetings last anywhere from 30 to 60 minutes. I always start them half an hour ahead of our start time, but when I was a floor supervisor with hourly employees, I'd start right at start time.

Staff Meetings

Now that the day-to-day business has a point of engagement— the daily meeting—next is the staff meeting. This meeting is about information and special topics when you want to have open discussion on key issues that impact your business and track your vision and performance. We will discuss how to have effective meetings in a subsequent chapter, but for now just know that the staff meeting is a course evaluation meeting: Are we on track for the goals? What are the key issues we need to discuss? This is where you can roll out any changes, discuss strategies, and debate topics.

> Staff meetings are course evaluation meetings to discuss whether you are on track to meet your goals and to talk about key issues.

A staff meeting is not everyone telling you what you should know about their department. That is important, but it is best done in a one-on-one meeting each week or every other week, depending on the state of the individual's area and your level of comfort or concern.

Staff meetings should last about two hours. They should take the place of the daily meeting on the day you hold them, and you should never cancel them.

Detailed Business Reviews

Finally, you need to pick a time of the month when you will do a detailed business review with your direct reports and at times (usually quarterly) their direct reports. This is a longer session—

half a day or a full day—in which you pore over the performance metrics in detail, make decisions, and ask for follow-up actions.

This is when you course-correct, plan advances, evaluate performance, and most importantly, listen and observe your team and how they run the business, react to issues, raise concerns, and export ideas. You should establish a monthly report cycle and have your business review the day after the monthly submissions are delivered so you are prepared and versed in the data.

Pick a time of the month to do a detailed business review with your direct reports and sometimes their direct reports.

Here again, the time and format of these meetings depends on the scale of your department or organization. But it doesn't really matter how large your department is—you still need to have a monthly review of how you are doing. Here, the managers or your staff tells you what the issues are and what they are doing about them.

One-on-One Communications

Finally, you need one-on-one time with your individuals. A weekly e-mail on the state of the business will help you in your weekly discussion—in fact, it can become the vehicle of your weekly discussion.

Make sure you have one-on-one time with your individuals.

When I ran a small department that did cost accounting in the '80s, I had each person write me a desk activity report, and I limited it to two paragraphs. Yes, they actually wrote it with a pen. (I am old!) There were four employees.

Each Friday, they would drop off the desk report as they left. I would read them, and on Monday at my huddle meeting, I would comment on any topics or things I saw in the report. At the time there was a spreadsheet application called Lotus 1-2-3 that was relatively new. Not everyone was well-versed in it, but we all had access to it on our desktop.

One of my accountants discovered a powerful feature called a *macro*, which was a serious of commands that, when strung together, could perform powerful calculations and would accept variable inputs. He mentioned this in his desk report, and that he thought he could automate our activity-based cost calculations. These took us forever to do, and we typically had to do them numerous times during our closing process as inventory levels changed and were finalized. The catch was that he needed to do this full time—he couldn't do anything else, and he figured he would need two weeks.

That Monday, I spoke about his update at the huddle meeting and said that if the team was willing to give it a shot, I would take on the desk myself for two weeks. We'd go for it, it would be huge if successful, and it would increase our accuracy, timeliness, and flexibility.

After the laughter died down about me actually doing the desk function, one of the team suggested a better way to do this. His suggestion was that we divide the workload among the three remaining members. They would put in the extra hours for two weeks, and I could be the QC person and the tester of the schedule—just like it was a real systems project.

Within two weeks we had the model done. We had issues with it and couldn't get some things to work, so we called the IBM help desk. (It was their product.) Finally, about six weeks later, we had it done! We were then able to instantaneously cost out our inventories—a process that took 4 people 12 hours was now done in 45 minutes.

You can only imagine what happened next. We began to automate everything we did with the same model, month after month, until we got the attention of the assistant controller, who could not believe the format, accuracy, and timeliness of our reports and the quality of our commentary on them. Now we actually analyzed and discussed the reports (and reviewed them)!

We began to get special projects sent to us, and we expanded the department to seven people. We hired in people who were very good at Lotus 1-2-3—that became a required skill in our area, and we produced. I moved into a larger area as a result of the unit's success, and all of the original four were promoted to different areas. We led the charge of automated schedules throughout the entire accounting area.

All this happened because people in my area were required to think and write down their thoughts and observations in a weekly desk report.

The same thing has happened in my career over and over again, by simply having people who report to me be required to tell me each week in writing what is on their minds. I am a CEO of a large organization, and all of my direct reports e-mail me an informal memo each week expressing what they are thinking about and what they are doing.

There just aren't enough pages in the book to tell you of all the success at all levels that I have seen born of the weekly update.

Now you have established all the input you need, you have scheduled your meetings, and you have scheduled the reports you will run the area with and which days they will come out—including every day. (Even if you work a day behind, that's okay, but have data.)

With all the input, you have now developed a system that will be driven by this information and will cause you to interact and manage. It will also cause all those who report to you to do the same.

Reports will come out, and people will read them and react to them. So all the reports must have data on them that serves the mission—they are the scoreboard.

A common error we all make as managers is that after we have defined the vision of where we want to be and the mission of how we will get there, we neglect to ask ourselves whether we are organized correctly to achieve these goals.

Remember that guy in my cost accounting department who had the better idea? Remember what it was about? Organization. We learned a long time ago, during the Industrial Revolution, that organizing people into an assembly line to produce a product was a good idea.

> Once you have a defined vision and a mission for how to get there, ask yourself whether you are organized correctly to achieve these goals.

This holds true in non-working life too. Think about it. On Saturdays we all have a set of chores we do—we go to the cleaners, do some grocery shopping, cut the lawn, and so on. The more chores you have, the more you benefit from organizing them in a sequence that allows you to complete them all in the course of the day. If you are passing the cleaners on the way to the grocery store, you may want to think about bringing the clothes with you to drop off—it makes you more efficient.

Managing a department or a company is no different; you need to be organized for the tasks that you need to accomplish, better known as your mission.

Roles and Responsibilities and Touch Points

Once you have the mission, you need to go through an organizational exercise that I call *roles and responsibilities and touch points*.

Create an organizational chart to define roles and responsibilities.

It starts with your current organizational chart. Going through the mission statement and the associated plan to accomplish it, you determine the role each area must play to accomplish the mission. Given that role, you assign the responsibility accordingly, and the net result is an organizational chart.

Next, you need to connect each area through touch points or interaction points that are clearly defined. It is only then that you are ready to run. More importantly, it is only then that you are ready to assess your talent and your performance.

Clearly defined touch points allow you to connect each area of your department to achieve your goals.

Let's explore how this works. Imagine you have been placed in charge of a call center. Customers call in each day with inquiries about their accounts, and your team provides the responses and service as well as cross-sells other products.

Your vision is to be "a competitive advantage," and your mission is to develop a customer experience that adds value by relieving anxiety customers may have and creating a feeling of confidence and personal service by delivering action-oriented solutions quickly and in a friendly manner.

Your current organizational structure looks like this: You have a call center team that answers the phones and attempts to resolve customer complaints. You have a research department that researches and resolves customer inquiries. You have a QC department that monitors all the work efforts to ensure compliance with procedures and policy. You have an escalation desk that handles all inquiries requiring subject matter expertise. Finally, you have a telephone center manager who monitors the technical equipment.

As your vision and mission evolve, you must continue to ask yourself whether you are organized correctly to achieve your goals.

Given the visions and the mission you have before you, is this the way you should be organized? That is the first question you must address, and you must continue to address it as the vision and mission become clearer and evolve. If the answer to the question is yes, you are ready (for now at least). If the answer is no, then you have to think about two things. First, what is the true north or the ideal organization to support the vision and mission? Second, what are the evolution time and the steps to get there? You don't just restructure with the same people and the same processes overnight.

So back to my question: Are you organized correctly for the mission?

I am guessing you are thinking no—and besides, what would I write about next if the answer was yes?

Let's dive into the thought process here for a moment and explore that a bit further. The very first thing is the vision—to become a competitive advantage. That means you need to do something in your call center that is better than your competition—perhaps it's different, but it clearly needs to be better.

The mission indicates that better is made up of a service that is action-oriented, friendly, fast, knowledgeable, and conveys confidence. Let's take a look at the path of a customer in your organization and see how that fits.

When a call comes in, your telephone area is the first point of interaction with the customer. Is that department delivering and monitoring the things that matter? How do they deliver speed, an anxiety-free experience, and confidence? Where do they get feedback on the customer experience and make adjustments? In this model, your telephone area needs to be more than technically adequate; they need to deliver a telephone experience consistent with the vision and the mission. The standalone vertical organizational structure seems to be the right structure because this requires highly specialized subject-matter expertise, but the touch points must be established so the information passes back and forth about the customer experience in such a way that adjustments can be made to ensure the mission.

Now you ask yourself a question: Is this the telephone area, or is this a customer access area? How you define an organization is one of the single largest influences on how people think about what they do. If you were the telephony manager, and I said to you that you were no longer the telephony manager, but that you were now the customer access manager, what would go through your mind? The obvious answer is a question: How else do customers access us? That may lead to web access, internal voice response systems, e-mail, and even text messaging. These are methods of speed and access that would allow customers 24/7 communication and relieve any worry any time, day or night.

Now you have the true north of the first area of your role. Typically, to get at this in a fashion that creates value in an organization, I would have a set of meetings with my direct reports and each department one by one to bounce the vision and mission up against the organizational structure and to get the ideas out on the table.

The next department is research. This is the area that researches the problems and works out the solutions. When you think of our mission, did the word *research* jump out at you? Speed, confidence, friendly, anxiety-free...and research! The fact of the matter is that some things require research, but in this mission, we need to minimize the anxiety during the research process, and we need to minimize the issues that require research. Every time we hand something off, our confidence level is threatened because we lose control of the transaction. In this scenario, we may want to combine research and the customer call center into one unit with the mission to drive down research time.

Having one group puts the problem in a different perspective; it's now aimed at the customer versus at one department or another. The customer solutions department, where we have the call center and research combined with a common goal of speed and minimized anxiety, will lead to interesting solutions in common with our mission. We may develop high-performance workstations where we empower the call center rep to do the research online and make the decision with the same tools the research department uses today.

I remember running a call center and reviewing all customer inquiries in the course of a month surrounding protested late fees on payments. This was a situation in which people paid a bill late for some reason; they were very good customers with excellent payment histories, but they just overlooked the bill or made a mistake of some kind. The process was that the call center representative would tell the customer that they would look into the matter and get back to them. They would send the "case" to our credit department, who would check the person's credit, and if the person had good credit rating, we would waive the late fee. The process took 48 hours—and that was improved, as it used to take 72 hours!

I looked at the data, and we averaged about 200 such cases a month—less than one percent of our calls. The 200 cases required that we handle 400 calls—the 200 asking the question and the 400 giving the answers—on our best performance in this process. Further, of the 200 cases we would handle, 99 percent of the cases resulted in a waved fee due to good credit. So, you ask, why couldn't the customer rep look up the credit screen and make the same decision? Well, the customer service department did not have access to credit information—that, of course, was in the credit department!

Touch points: Where do departments cross over, what is the path of your customer, and how does it relate to the mission? We gave the customer service representative access to that one screen and created the rules and policies, and the calls became 60-second transactions with happy customers who were handled completely the first time they called in 99 percent of the time!

In our hypothetical organizational structure, research needs to be reworked as a separate area because by definition it clashes with the mission. That does not mean we shouldn't research things; it means that research cannot be a standalone area because it has the potential to become an obstacle if it stands alone.

Now there is the matter of customer escalation—when the process doesn't work and the customer wants to opt out of it. If you have a department for this, the first question you have to ask is how big of a problem do you have? A small presidential complaint area for handling complaints directed to the president or executive management is typical, but I would challenge the area to make itself obsolete. Every time they solve something, two things are true: The process didn't work in the line, and the presidential complaint area has empowerment that the line doesn't.

You need to ask yourself in this construct whether that is okay. The answer could be yes, but escalation is sourced by breakdowns, so where are you monitoring breakdowns?

You have a quality control department, and they should be monitoring all breakdowns and improving the process with their feedback. So you might think about whether you could combine the QC and escalation units and focus on process improvements and problem resolution in one area.

As you can see, the organizational structure is key to your ability to execute the mission and assess your talent, but many managers just come in and start managing without even thinking about the organizational structure. Later, they find out through experience that they may need to restructure to improve things, but they often have dug the hole by then, and it could be too deep. Reorganizations are disruptive and create lower productivity initially, so you want to be mindful and thoughtful in the approach. You clearly need to do the exercise here to see what the end game will be. Start down the path to move it there by adding the talent and defining the touch points and interdependencies, validating that they need to exist (like the credit screen!) and establishing expectations where they have to exist.

> Organizational structure is key to executing the mission and assessing your talent.

> Reorganizations are disruptive and create lower productivity initially, so be thoughtful in your approach.

You may also identify areas where you do not have the talent in house. Can the telephony person become the web person quickly enough for you to succeed?

Once you've defined the organizational structure, you need to list the functions for each role.

Once you have the organizational structure defined—those are the roles—the next thing you need to do is list out all the functions you do under each role in the organizational chart. That clearly defines the responsibilities, and you'll be surprised by how many people do the same thing or slightly overlap. You will find areas that have morphed out of need and areas that should have gone away in the last re-org but that no one wanted to take on. The org chart should span the page with the department names, and underneath each department the responsibilities should be listed, because departments have multiple responsibilities (see Figure 2.1).

Figure 2.1
A sample organizational chart.

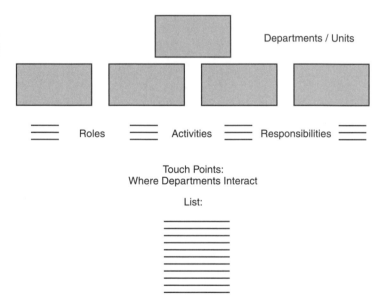

Once you've defined the roles and responsibilities, you must address the touch points.

Once you lay out the responsibilities across the organization and verify that the responsibilities are defined and in the correct spots, you have a clear understanding of who does what, and so do the leaders of those units if you reviewed the information collectively. The next questions are what are the touch points and what are the rules of engagement on those touch points?

I will give you an example. When I did the exercise a few years back with all of my directs, we discovered we had two project management organizations in the company. The information technology group had a project management department (PMO), and the operations area had a project management group. Also, each individual area had a person or two (or three) with the title of project manager. In total, out of about 8,000 people—of which 4,500 were in sales and service delivery, 2,000 were in customer service, and 1,500 were in support—280 were project managers!

And of course we struggled because we couldn't get anything done!

What could have been the problem? Touch points. We had people, and they had roles and responsibilities, but they didn't understand or perhaps even know how they fit together or how they came together to make something happen.

We spent the next six weeks modeling how a project should work and vetted it with the project management teams themselves. We decided which projects should be managed centrally, which should be done within a department, what a project manager's job was, what tools we would give them to use, what reports and controls we needed, and what the career path and qualifications of a project manger should be. The result was that we became very good at getting things done—we did them once, and we did them quickly. Downstream issues that were prevalent in the old structure due to lack of coordination among teams went away, and as a result we improved the interaction between departments as well.

These were all byproducts of the organization and the roles, responsibilities, and touch points exercise.

Here again, I have to emphasize that all of this activity happens simultaneously, and it comes together at different points in time. But as a manager, you need to be working on the vision, mission, values, and organizational structure to best position you to achieve the vision. Finally, you must assess the talent that you have within the context of all of these as you run the day-to-day business.

> You must work on the vision, mission, values, and organizational structure to best position you to achieve your vision.

Having a Plan

All this would overwhelm you if you did not have a plan. That is the issue I see over and over again in management—the manager doesn't have a roadmap of where he or she is going.

As a manager, you must have a roadmap of where you are going!

Imagine if I told you to meet me in Chicago at two o'clock this next Tuesday. Could you do it? Impossible. Chicago is a rather large place filled with many people and buildings; you simply don't have the information you need to execute this.

Suppose I told you to meet me there at two o'clock, on the corner of Michigan and Huron, in front of the hotel. Now you can be there. Imagine you go there, and I have on a tuxedo and tell you we are going to a black-tie awards dinner at two o'clock. Would you be ready?

That is often how managing is—you get bits and pieces of information because your inclination is to act, but the fact of the matter is that the best managers have a plan of where they are going and understand why they need to be there before they take the first step.

Managers create systems that reinforce what they have to do to achieve success.

Then they create management systems that reinforce the things they have to do in order to achieve success. Activities, interactions, meetings, data gathering and analysis, and action—all designed to get to the goal, the vision. Through the repetition of the system, they perfect and perfect until their organization runs nearly flawlessly and repeatedly achieves the objectives they set out to do.

Managing Horizontally

Managing horizontally refers to reviewing one aspect of a business across all business units; managing vertically refers to reviewing all aspects of a business unit within that unit.

When I ran my first large organization, I had more than 1,000 people who reported to me; prior to that, the most I ever had reporting to me was 200 people. It's not so much the body count, but rather the number of things or the scope for which you are responsible that drives the complexity. It was then that I decided to begin to manage horizontally more than vertically. What that means is, instead of reviewing all aspects of a business unit within that unit, I would review one aspect of the business across all business units.

So, I would have a meeting to review operational risk, and all business unit leaders, auditors, and quality control would come together, and we would review across the organization our risk performance. The control groups would report out, the business units would address issues, and I would get a common view of all risk across the organization. The attendees would get to share best practices and understand solutions and issues that might impact their units one day. It served as radar for the units because they got to hear and see all the other units' issues, and in doing so they were able to ask themselves whether it could happen to them. We met and evaluated risk on the third Thursday of every month from 2 to 4 p.m. It was the same agenda: auditors reviewed the audits in progress and the completed reports since the last meeting, quality control reported out the results of their testing by area, and then each area reported out their remediation plans, audit follow-ups, and reactions to the current reports they heard.

This meeting and its agenda created a mindset around risk; people set deadlines for responses, issue resolution, and so on based on the third Thursday of the month. Meetings were held for clarity of issues and conflicts prior to that meeting so people were on the same page when they attended. Areas would provide help and support based on the expertise they had. If an approach worked great to mitigate an audit issue, we adopted it across the organization.

But something else was happening, too. As the manager, I got to see the people in action, get a sense for the talent we had in risk management, and understand how people approached deadlines and how they interacted and conducted themselves, all the while assessing their capability to achieve the mission and the vision. In addition, we were looking at the control breaks to shore up the execution within the organizational structure. If an audit failure was the result of everyone doing what they were supposed to, that was an organizational or process issue; if no one had the responsibility, then that was clearly an organizational issue.

Navigating Obstacles

As you run the day-to-day business, after going through the initial steps of vision, mission, and values and the organizational structure, defining the roles and responsibilities and touch points, you will see two things begin to happen. First, you will see the evolution of the organization toward the vision. Second, you will see the obstacles, and you will begin the navigation process that is management.

As you begin to see the evolution of your organization toward the vision, you will also see the obstacles and begin the navigation process that is management.

In 1990, I took over the management of a large organization in the financial services industry that, among other things, managed mortgage defaults. The Northeast had just gone through a massive equity correction, and the financial crisis in real estate had begun, with credit defaults and foreclosures. The troubled times of the economy had exacerbated an already worsening condition.

We went through the steps of the vision, mission, and values process; we reviewed our understanding of the organization and the structure; and we had a plan. The plan was to mitigate the losses that were projected to be some $300 million, return the organization to a state of readiness for when the market bounced back, and put in controls and processes throughout to better manage our platform.

The management team had gotten very careless in their approach to running the day-to-day business and had created too many layers of management to really direct the activities of the changing environment as quickly and flexibly as perhaps they needed to. In addition, the team I took over had been in place for a few years, had their own way of doing things, and were not very open to change.

The process of focus groups and discussions on organizational structure were somewhat intimidating to the team, but I never managed from the floor or overreacted to what I saw and heard. They were all data points that I was gathering, synthesizing, and playing back to the management team to engage them in finding solutions to issues and delivering back solutions as a team.

As the first months unfolded in that organization, there was a department that was the example of how this all comes together—the collections department.

My first morning meeting was a signal for all of us. It started at 7:30 a.m., but there was one problem—there were only two direct reports and me in the room at 7:30 a.m. I began the meeting. One value we all agreed on was respect, and as I began the meeting, I said, "It's 7:30 a.m. I respect your time as managers, so we will begin." As the updates began, the remaining people began to enter the room at various times—some would apologize for being late, while others just sat down. At one point, one of the stragglers attempted to say something and started with, "You may have already covered this; I was late, but..." I interrupted him: "We did cover it, so you'll have to wait until tomorrow. We have a limited time in this meeting."

It was a shock to everyone that we were actually going to run the meeting the way we said we would! When it came time for the collections update, the manager started with, "We don't have any real daily MIS that can summarize everything, so I thought I would just give you guys a verbal update."

After his update concluded, I spoke. "We agreed we would have a daily management statistics report for each area. One of our values was teamwork, another integrity, and a third respect. When we agree on something, I need you to do it in the context of those values. I expect we will have MIS each day and it will develop over time. If you are struggling with it, then see me and I can help, but you cannot simply decide you will not live up to an agreement after it is made among us—no one can, not even me."

The second day at 7:30 a.m., there were 10 people around the table, and two who had been late the day before were absent as we began. I have mentioned that as a manager, your job is to assess talent and interaction and in the next 90 days choose a team that will allow you to achieve your vision. You collect data points and constantly need to ask yourself what they tell you about your ability to achieve the vision? The absence of two key players for the second day in a row at the start of the meeting said a few things to me. It spoke of their understanding or commitment to the values and their commitment to the management processes as well.

These are the discussion points you want to collect so you can then sit down and have an open conversation as to what is happening with people like this, but you need to give them some time. On the second day, the collections manager had MIS, and we looked at his indicators versus the goals we had set. Every indicator has to have an end goal, what is defined as success, a forecast that says the time it will take to get there, and the trend line to see whether you are getting there. The end goal needs to reflect the vision state.

It was about Day 6 when we had our first real meeting. I walked into the room at 7:25 a.m. to find everyone there. Relentless repetition had sunk in, and they were all talking to each other about something. I called the meeting together.

The collections MIS had shown that we were falling behind in our collection calls, so I asked what the issue was. The first response was that this was normal and no issues needed to be addressed—it was just one of those things. We had a holiday the week before and some people were out, so we just didn't have the right staff levels. I asked what we would need to do to keep this from happening again. What would we need to track, manage, decide, and so on in order for us never to trend backward in collection calls?

The response was weak. After the meeting the collection manager came to see me. "Look, Tony, if I am not the guy you want managing this area, just let me know. But if I am, then you have to trust me and how I manage."

I replied, "Well we agreed to manage quantitatively as a team and use the MIS to help us direct and manage activity and further keep score of our progress, so this has nothing to do with trust and everything to do with managing. Tell me what your plan is and then I will trust you to execute it. If you don't tell me, I have nothing to trust. As for whether you are the guy, I cannot tell you if you are or are not from a few days' worth of interaction with you. I need to see where we go as a team and how you fit on that team and play with that team."

His response was very telling to me, and something that has remained with me for a long time, even until this day. He looked at me quizzically and said, "You really believe this stuff, don't you?"

As you read this book and hopefully reflect on this method of management, the most important thing you can do is understand this approach, accept it, and believe in it, because each one of your people will need to do the same, and it is not a common way to think about managing. Oh, the words are familiar enough, but the applications of the methods, particularly on a universal basis, are not at all common, and they will constantly be challenged.

After the shock wore off in a few seconds, I said, "Of course I believe in it. Do you?" He told me he didn't really understand it all and how it was all coming together, but from that morning's conversation, he understood that it indeed was the path we were going on, and he wanted to know more so he could be one of those leaders at the end.

As a manager, you must constantly talk about the vision, the mission, and how you are going about them.

This is an example of the entire system at work—the daily business issues, the values, the mission, and the data points all working to help you assess and manage the talent to achieve the goal. The collections manager became the first student of what we were trying to do, and he helped perfect the process and enable the team in ways I could never have contributed.

You have to constantly talk about the vision, the mission, and the way you are going about them. You have to use the values and explicitly call people's attention to the fact that this is how you are making decisions and running the business. That way, they can emulate the behaviors and incorporate them into their work and develop their personal style accordingly.

Each day as you run the system, you will be extracting data, evaluating people, making decisions, and moving the entire company or department along in the direction you want. The key to success is to be aware and to make adjustments and keep interacting at every point in the process.

That is an example of a management system approach and how you, as the manager, must keep your plan in front of you and be aware to take in the data that you need to achieve it at every point in the system.

Chapter 3

Change

In the next 90 days, as you begin to refine and manage with a whole new approach and an entire new level of engagement and interaction that will lead to great success, one thing is certain: It will mean change.

Dealing with change is a key ingredient of any manager's toolkit, and there have been more books and seminars written on change and change management than probably any other topic. The reason is that no one has really cracked the code on how to make an effective change. My conclusion is that the real issue is not that people don't want to embrace change—an assumption all the change agents and experts go in with.

Why Do People Resist Change?

In the book *Good to Great*, Jim Collins tells us the enemy of great is good. Collins theorizes that if you are good—*really* good—at what you do, you are lured into a false sense of security and are no longer externally motivated to improve. And, because improvement often requires change, people naturally resist even when there is a compelling reason to change. You see, the presupposition is that no one really likes to or wants to change. I do not believe that to be the case.

So, the first thing I would like you to consider about being a better manager is that good performance or a comfort zone comes from complacency. If you give people a reason to change, and they accept that reason, they will embrace change, no matter what their performance is like or what their accomplishments may be.

> If you give people a reason to change, and they accept that reason, they will embrace change, no matter what their performance is like or what their accomplishments may be.

It is awareness and capability that cause people to change, and people who do not change behavior don't avoid change because they are resistant or dislike it, but rather because they were not aware of the need to change or they do not have the capability or tools to change.

Let's face it: No one wants to fail in life. No one says on the way to work each day, "I hope I get fired—my goal is to fail." On the contrary, we are taught from day one to seek approval, praise, and recognition for our actions as human beings. Everyone is looking for that promotion or raise or reward. So, if change is needed to achieve that reward, recognition, and praise, people will indeed embrace it—it is our natural tendency as humans!

So why don't people embrace change, especially change that will position them for greater success? Two reasons: First, they do not realize or see the need to change; they do not believe the change will help them. In a word, they are unaware. The second reason is that while they may have known, understood, and accepted the need for change, they were not capable of making the change.

If change is needed to achieve reward, recognition, and praise, people will embrace it.

Articulating the Need for Change

As a manager, you must make people aware of the change, have them accept the need to change, help them understand it, and then give them the capability in the form of tools to make the change. We have all had that same experience of asking a stranger on the street for directions, only to find out that they do not speak our language. Our reaction is always the same; we ask the question again, only louder this time, in the hope that the increased volume will allow the person to understand us.

A manager must make people aware of change, have them accept the need to change, help them understand it, and then give them the tools to make it.

The person is incapable of understanding us and will remain incapable unless we teach them the language or find some other means of communicating with them to get to the same goal. Obviously, when the person woke up in the morning that day, he didn't realize that mastering the English language was going to be a requirement of the day!

Unless you make the case for a change as you describe your vision, mission, and values, and unless people understand the potential result of achieving the vision and how it will impact each of them, you are only talking louder. That is why it is a process to manage people, and it is a daily process to create an environment using a management system in which success is a natural outcome. Too many times we jump to capability and begin with that as our focus. This complicates the change and potentially confuses people as to why we are changing in the first place.

It is a daily process to manage people and create an environment using a management system in which success is a natural outcome.

Often people don't understand why they need to change. But if they do, they often not only participate, but end up leading and accelerating the change. And you will find that many times they were fully capable of change in the first place. I have a friend who is a captain for an airline. Now, we have all heard the preflight announcement on planes asking us to shut down all our communications equipment, electronic devices, and anything with an on/off switch. To my amazement, many people don't adhere to

If people understand the need to change, they often not only participate, but they end up leading the change.

the request. But on my friend's flights, they always do. As his plane taxies out to the runway, he always comes on and says, "Ladies and gentlemen, from the cockpit I can tell that some of you have not shut off your electronic equipment. The problem is that the electronic signals may interfere with our communications and/or signals here in the cockpit as we take off, so please shut them down." He always tells of people literally scrambling after that announcement to comply. Why? Awareness.

Change without awareness and capability happens, but it is dangerous because it is procedural and at times robotic or without thought. You see this with a new title, process, or position all the time. In these cases the change defines us versus us defining the change, and that doesn't allow the change to be internalized or developed. As a result, the change narrows people, process, and activity and narrows the potential impact it may have had in achieving the vision or mission.

We should define the change, rather than the change defining us.

Remember, people want to and will try to achieve what is expected of them—that's why you need to communicate the thought process so they can live the spirit of the vision, not merely the words. A number of years ago I was going Christmas shopping for my son, who wanted a Chicago Cubs jersey. (Great kid, but not a good judge of baseball teams!) It was December 23rd; I had waited a bit long to ensure his request was legitimate, being a Yankees fan myself.

In any event, my shopping experience is living proof that unless people internalize the vision and fully understand what you are trying to achieve, they cannot and do not deliver. As I hurried into Sears to look for the jersey, hoping I didn't wait too long—after all, I was living in Chicago at the time—I quickly raced to the boys department and began to frantically look for the jersey. I spotted it—Ryan Sandberg, his favorite player, and the correct size. Done!

I'm not sure whether you have ever shopped in Sears, but like many department stores, it operates with large areas or departments in sections. Having secured the merchandise, I began to walk around and look for a checkout counter.

If you have been to a Sears store, you may have encountered the fact that while there is a large selection, plenty of floor space, and many departments, sometimes there seem to be no cashiers at any of the registers. Such was the case on this evening. To exacerbate my problem, the store was closing at 9 p.m., and it was about 8:45 p.m.

I began to look for a cashier, walking from department to department. In no department did I find a cashier. Then I saw something in the distance that amounted to a ray of hope a Sears employee! I knew she was a Sears employee because she had a lanyard on that said SEARS in large letters. Further, it said *Customer Service Department*. I quickly began to move toward her. She was heading my way, so it was an easy chase. As we got closer and closer, I lined myself up so we would meet in the aisle and then finally, when we were about four feet apart, I spoke.

"Excuse me. I am trying to buy this jersey for my son, and I cannot seem to find a cash register. I was wondering if you could check me out or help me out here."

She looked at me and said," I am sorry, sir. I cannot help you— I am in customer service."

True story! A story that lives in my mind as a reminder that when you define people and roles versus giving them an understanding of what you are trying to achieve, they will do exactly what you ask of them, nothing more and perhaps nothing less. Helping and servicing people must have had a very narrow definition that Christmas season. There was little room for creativity and interpretation—customer service meant something very specific, and it didn't mean checking people out or helping them find a checkout station that was open.

Had the vision been "we make our customers' experience a positive one" and had roles been defined underneath that with possible touch points, my story would have had a much different ending. However, it is obvious that was not the way the vision was communicated, if it was communicated at all.

Communicating Change

The problem with change sometimes is that people allow the change to define them versus incorporating themselves into the change—a subtle but important point. It's funny, people who never followed the rules and practices to the letter before suddenly go literal on you during change because they want to get it correct. The reason why they do what they are told is often because that is *all* they are told. They are not aware of why they are changing in the first place. When they are aware of why they are changing, that becomes their motivation for seeking the capability. And when they are capable, they can accept change and then they can internalize it, own it, and grow and develop it.

You see, I don't believe people do not want to embrace change. I believe they cannot embrace change until they are aware of why the change is needed in the first place. Once they understand that change is needed, then they must prepare themselves to become capable of making the change. As a result, they internalize it. This is when change catches on, and the department or organization begins to make the move collectively.

Change is about three things:

1. Awareness

2. Capability

3. Internalization

The problem is that all of us in business and even in education—in fact, in any organized profession—go to Number 2 immediately and focus on the change. Then we measure the effectiveness of things like training and implementation plans and make judgments about attitude, morale, and execution. In senior management, we forget that by the time the new process, product, policy, vision, mission, and so on rolls out, we have discussed it for months, debated it endlessly, vetted it, understood it, and internalized it, and we expect everyone to be on the same page without any benefit of time in reading the book!

As you begin to execute your new vision, mission, and values, you will need to define for people over and over again what they mean and how they are different from what people do already. You have to show people the value of achieving that vision, and you have to point out the progress and the failures along the way. The management system will drive points of interaction toward you, and you must field them in a manner that always reinforces what you are trying to achieve. You must take the time to explain how to connect the dots so people can take the vision and run with it.

You cannot be over-prescriptive, or you will wind up with the customer service rep who can't help a customer because she is in customer service. When I ran a customer service unit in the '90s, we wanted to alleviate anxiety in the process, and we determined from our customer surveys that the way to do this was to communicate with our customers all along the process of fulfilling their order. One of my managers in sales came to our morning meeting with a suggestion that we should implement a procedure in which our sales force would contact our customers four hours after they placed an order with us. That way, we would be in touch with the customer.

Sounds like a good idea, but let's look at it a bit more closely. The practice or policy doesn't say the purpose of the contact. What exactly are we trying to achieve? Often in these types of practices driven only by a time metric, the result is a checking-the-box mentality rather than really making a difference, because the reason you are executing the process is unknown. Moreover, you are executing because you have to. As we discussed this suggestion further, we began to ask how this would help us achieve the mission of providing superior service and relieving anxiety. That led to a refinement that we would call the customer within the first eight hours after they placed an order to assure them that we had received the order and they were in good hands, and to verify the key points of information and set the expectations for the delivery. Now people understood why we were contacting the customer, what we would do, and how it fit into the mission. They then could internalize the service and have the conversation with the intent that was meant. They would have a better relationship with the customer and would develop trust in the relationship, and this would likely lead to a better experience and ultimately better service and more business for the company.

We changed from not contacting the customer unless there was a problem to contacting the customer within the first eight hours of every order to ensure the process and alleviate anxiety in it. People understood that our vision was to deliver superior service, and the mission included this action because it supported the vision. If we executed it, we would all succeed.

People ran with the concept, contacted customers, and solved all types of issues at the first checkpoint. There were issues and problems we never intended to address at that first contact, but the mission was to alleviate the anxiety, so when we saw anxiety in the process, we jumped on it.

If the mission had been to make the call or even the contact, it would have been over the minute we spoke to the customer; we would have checked the box and moved on. But people internalized the change. They knew what was at stake—we had to improve our service level. They understood why it was important from the customer's view, and we had presented the same research that we reviewed in the boardroom to them. As a result, they got it and ran with it.

Our customer service scores improved dramatically, and we didn't stop with just one change. People began to see how we could become anxiety-free throughout the process, but the model was the first contact call. Its success paved the way for continuous improvement throughout.

Modeling and Reviewing Change

Modeling change and reviewing its successes and failures gives your employees a meaningful example of your expectations and reinforces all the aspects of your vision, mission, and values in a tangible way.

People need to see change to emulate it and carry it forward.

When people see the change, they can emulate it, carry it forward, and support it, but the fact is they need to see it. As the manager, you need to point it out and connect it all for them.

One of the tools I always use in the midst of changing a cultural or workplace environment is to periodically survey the group and ask, "In the last *x* months [weeks, and so on], name something that has changed." The results are remarkable as well as insightful, and they serve as a guidepost.

It can be helpful to survey your group about changes.

I recall running such a survey in one of my groups six months after we rolled out our vision, mission, and values. We were rocking, things were moving, the management team had embraced the new interactions, daily meetings were producing results, and we thought life was just grand. We ran the survey and planned to show the results at the monthly town hall as part of the report card on how we were doing. Having a monthly management report card to share publicly with your employees really keeps the management team focused and the employees engaged.

We received about 40 responses from the random 50 surveys with the one question about naming one thing that had changed in the past few months. Of the 40 responses, about 30 were positive, about 7 were neutral, and the remaining 3 were variations on the word *nothing*.

The management team was devastated, especially by the three "nothing" responses. Thirty out of 40 was 75 percent—a

C grade—and the team had worked very hard in the past few months. This is a point that every one of us as managers must face. It is a point where your feedback doesn't meet your expectations. It is a point that can often challenge your strategy, your tactics, and even your personal energy or morale. And here is a fact—it should. That is what feedback is supposed to do — it is supposed to make you feel all of those things that will lead you to the next logical step in the improvement process. Otherwise, what value does it have?

My team began a rationalization process: "We surveyed at the end of the month," "The systems were down that day," "People just don't understand what we have done," "We need to tell them how good the place is becoming," and my favorite—"If they don't like it, they should just leave!"

Here is my rule on feedback: Feedback always correctly represents the perception of those giving it. Now make the decision to deal with the perception or let it evolve. Let me give you an example. Together with my wife of 30+ years, I have raised three children that I could not be more proud of, and I am sure at times in the Meola house they may have questioned everything from my love for them, to my fairness, to my parenting skills. I think I can point out a few of those times when the feedback was pretty clear that the children I was raising doubted my judgment. There were times when I took the time to explain my rationale, thoughts, and behavior in great detail, and there were other times when, abiding by the advice of my lovely wife, I just—in the words of Paul McCartney—"let it be."

> Feedback always correctly represents the perception of those giving it.

Choosing Your Battles

As a manager, you cannot run around trying to address everything, making the world perfect for your employees. As with kids, there are times when employees have to come to their own conclusions and seek information from sources other than you and your management team. The trick is to know which time is which.

If you are dealing with an issue of values, it must be met and dealt with head on. Values are the core of your environment, and they need to be managed, explained, and dealt with in a manner that always reinforces them.

Issues of values must be met and dealt with head on.

Dealing with the mission and vision may take time to evolve, particularly when execution is the issue. Trial and error and evolution are the ways you perfect execution, and by definition you will have some false starts.

Finally, a rule of thumb that I picked up years ago as a teenager in Bible Study applies to the largest-scale management roles in corporate America: If it is not working against you, then it is working for you.

If it is not working against you, then it is working for you.

Let me explain that a bit more. One of the things that my team lamented in the feedback was the fact that one of the positive changes read, "We have staff meetings now," and one of the negative comments was, "Our staff meetings are a waste of time." Yet another was, "We still don't have staff meetings."

They wanted to go to work on this immediately, fueled by the fact that they had come to actually like and value our daily staff meetings—a meeting people felt wasn't needed, was a waste of time, and for which they couldn't fathom what we would talk about every single day!

I asked a simple question. "We have gone from an organization that had hardly any staff meetings to now having some staff meetings and focusing on the quality of staff meetings in a short period of time without a special focus or project or activity. Why do you think we moved the needle from zero to here?" No one could give me a specific answer to the question. There were theories, suggestions, and opinions, but no one could logically explain what had happened over the months to bring us to a point where we were not only having staff meetings, suddenly we were trying to improve them!

Staff meetings are part of a management system that reinforces the vision, mission, and values.

Remember when I talked about creating a management system that reinforces the vision, mission, and values early on? Well, staff meetings are part of that system. When you, as a manager of managers, have a daily staff meeting, suddenly there is a need to disseminate information to others in the organization, mainly because people have information, they have direction, and they need and want to communicate it. Add the fact that they have goals and the information will help them attain those goals, and they not only *need* to disseminate the information, they *want* to disseminate it because they will be more successful for having done so!

The fact that staff meetings suddenly were popping up was evidence that we were transforming from a silo organization with no communications to an organization in dialogue—it was proof that our values of respecting people's opinions, communicating, and promoting teamwork were taking hold. Our decision was not whether to help managers have better staff meetings or to require managers to have them, it was how to reinforce the positive activity. When you have positive activity aligned with your vision, mission, and values, it is incumbent on you, the manager, to recognize the behavior so that others can model it.

When you have positive activity aligned with your vision, mission, and values, you must recognize the behavior so others can model it.

We chose to let the staff-meeting wave continue on its own, but to incorporate and reinforce staff meetings in our system and our communications. We would end all employee bulletins with the sentence, "Please raise and questions and concerns about this announcement at your next staff meeting." We also opened up a web-line for managers referencing any announcement, where the employees could submit a question and not only get the answer to it, but also have access to frequently asked questions and responses.

Nearly six months after our first feedback at a town hall, I spoke about the importance of staff meetings, how I hoped my managers were having them, and that they were helpful sessions to have. I was interrupted by extemporaneous and thunderous applause.

You don't have to chase everything. There are many things that you simply need to let evolve, and having a timeline that equates to your plan will allow you to decide when to act and when to allow evolution and simply monitor the progress.

There are many things that you simply need to let evolve.

As you begin to see changes and manage the changes in your department that will ultimately lead you to achieve your mission and values, there will be people, processes, and technology whose behaviors to date—specifically, the way they operated—may not fit the new direction.

Handling these situations in accordance with your values is the key. In an organization where a value might be respect or integrity, you have to be mindful that these aspects of the department worked in a different time and a different era. There is never anything to be gained by criticizing the past. Believe me, there were smart people before you, and there will be smart people after you. So your questions, comments, and behaviors ought to simply be focused on the here and now. History is an input for you, not a benchmark or a standard you must justify the existence of or your deviation from—use it in that manner.

In management, there is nothing to gain by criticizing the past.

The Formula of Change

A vision is far-reaching, and if you are relentless in its pursuit, then you will change and affect many pieces of the department in many aspects, situations, and ways. In the customer service department I mentioned, where we were all about relieving the anxiety of the transaction, one of the things we had to deal with was the timing of the applications that updated our systems.

If we were truly going to be able to put customers at ease when they contacted us, we had to have up-to-the-moment information available to us. In turn, that meant revamping the technology production schedule—a schedule that had not changed in any substantive manner in 10 years! You can imagine the anxiety we felt as we discovered that our vision pointed us to this task, and this task was not easy, inexpensive, or without risk.

It is crucial that people understand the vision and mission so they can apply it in their area of expertise.

This is why it is so pivotal that people understand the vision and the mission, so that in their area of expertise they can apply it. I learned on our technology project that there were certain systems that had a direct impact on the customer, meaning the customer inquiries were always answered within these modules, and others where the customer data was seldom accessed. I also learned that our system's production schedule was centered around the accounting department's schedule, not operations or the customer experience. Those areas were thought of as secondary in determining which technology job went to the queue next.

In an environment where getting the accounting accurate and timely was paramount, then our schedule was spot on target, but in an environment where we wanted an anxiety-free customer, that wouldn't be the way to make the decision. So, I asked the technology team what we should do, given our mission and our vision, to line up our technology efforts so the system supported the vision.

"Does our technology support the vision?" is the type of question that sparks change, versus saying, "We need to change our technology to support the vision." The latter is more of a conclusion that you reach, but the technology people may or may not understand your thought process, even after you explain it.

The tech team came back with a compete analysis of why we needed to overhaul our approach to technology, complete with the budget request to do it! The important point was that I had engaged them, and the things they were looking at and needed to change were things that, frankly, I never would have thought about. They were all right on point and in line with our vision—a vision that the tech team now understood and could relate to in a way they could not have if they hadn't gone through the thought process to determine what the vision meant to them and their individual roles.

They were aware of why we needed to change, they were capable, and now they had internalized it. That continues to be the formula of change.

I have made the point several times that these practices are not only for CEOs; they pertain to any manager in any situation. When you are managing a group, part of what you will inevitably do is change something. So far we have talked about the mindset of change, which is 50 percent of the equation—the remaining 50 percent deals with the process of change.

> The mindset of change is 50 percent of the equation; the process of change is the other 50 percent.

The Process of Change

To effectively change a process, procedure, practice, or behavior of any sort, clearly understanding why you are making the change, as I have noted, is paramount. But then what?

There are five steps to making an operational change:

1. Review the end-to-end process to identify all dependencies and downstream changes.
2. Quantify the changes.
3. Test the changes.
4. Train for the new behaviors required.
5. Validate.

Every operational change starts with the question, "What changes?" The only way to know what will change is to truly know what the current state is—not always an easy task. You may have written policies and procedures, but there are everyday practices—workarounds that are not always obvious when you look at a manual or chart. That is why you need to review and create a process map—a high-level, end-to-end document that needs to be reviewed with the team that will execute the change and at least one representative from any of the downstream or impacted departments. There are those who will actually change the process and activity of what they do, and there will be those who simply

> To make an operational change, you must review the process, quantify and test the changes, train for the new behaviors, and then validate the outcome.

need to know about the change but will take no action. And, there will be those areas that will have to adjust what they do because you have adjusted what you do. Finally, there is the information and data that flows out of a change in process that will potentially change anything from data structure to data definition, and there is a set of people that need to know that as well.

Reviewing the End-to-End Process to Identify All Dependencies and Downstream Changes

In the early part of 2003, I was running the mortgage business for a well-known bank that happened to be the leader in Montage originations at the time. One of the things we were dealing with was the phenomenal growth in business that we were experiencing and, frankly, keeping up with it all. The guys in secondary marketing who had to trade all the assets we originated were constantly requiring changes in the way we viewed and categorized certain information related to loan data. They would be negotiating a deal, and the buyer would say something like, "I want to eliminate all loans with these parameters from the bid—so what would that look like?" Of course, they would immediately call our MIS department and start screaming, as traders do, that they needed this information ASAP. To complicate matters, they never got the request quite right out of the chute, and we had a production system that required inquiries of this type and magnitude to be done overnight.

My MIS manager, faced with this constant Groundhog Day dilemma, thought of a solution that would make life easier for everyone. He would create some generic groupings—or *pools*, as we called them on the system. Then, when traders would call, 80 percent of the info would be there in real time, and that would be good enough for an indicative price on a buy. We would follow up with the next-day balancing out, and—bingo!—we would have the final pricing. You don't have to know mortgages to know that real-time response in a negotiation is good, and being able to do things once versus numerous times is even better.

To create this little masterpiece, my manager needed to label each loan record. But getting a new field in a system is a bit like discovering new geography in the world—it isn't very easy because it is all being used, and God just isn't making land anymore! So the team decided to scour the data dictionary, find a field that wasn't being used for anything, and use it for their label. In the confines of their cubicles, after producing reams of data dumps, they did just that—they found a field that was empty on every record on every loan in the system. The field title was called *stop code*, and yes, this is a true story!

Within two days they had done all their labeling and developed a program that would populate the stop code with their labels. The inquiry programs would use the code in a dynamic fashion so that the traders could do their jobs in real time, still screw up communications, and recover instantly when they did. Too good to be true—yes indeed, too good to be true.

The morning after the program ran was exciting. Everything worked as planned, the codes were in, and we could slice and dice that data on a moment's notice. In fact, we ran a few test cases just for good measure, and the load of the labels and the reports were just awesome. And for good measure, we were pounding our collective chest that we did this without all the bureaucracy of project management, information technology, and tons of meetings and debates. We just did it—sort of like Nike! It was a proud moment in that MIS department, and the traders just loved it!

It was about 10:00 when the head of IT called me with the newest major crisis of the day. None of our systems were showing any loan-level detail. None of them—not finance, not accounting, not credit, not service, and not even the trade room. No daily loads updated the loan-level files. He wanted to assure me that we could simply use yesterday's master file, "append" new production, and be back in business at about noon, and they could simultaneously try to figure out what happened. I, of course, novice master of technology, asked the usual great IT question that one asks when something goes wrong: "Did we implement any system changes last night?"

Of course, we looked at the change control log that documents any changes to any system and it was blank, so the answer was no. It was about 1:00 when the replacement files came up with everything loaded, and life was good except for one little area—MIS.

The MIS manager was furious; the new files contained no labels because they were made up of yesterday morning's history files and just customer transactions (our appended data). He rushed into the IT manager's office to inform him that the reload was not only unsuccessful, but it had destroyed more than three days' worth of work, and the traders were not going to be happy!

It is crucial to review the end-to-end process that a change will impact to understand all the implications of the change.

After sorting through what I could only describe as one of the most convoluted discussions I have witnessed between those two managers, we had found our issue. It seems that the stop code field was there for use by IT to prevent loans from feeding any loan-level file. It was a binary field, meaning if it was not blank the system stopped the feed, and if it was blank the system let the loan pass to the loan-level detail file. This field was used primarily when we tested programs and was only used by IT—until this week, when our MIS crew decided to use it.

Understanding the end-to-end implications of a change seems logical in hindsight, but it is a basic fundamental of change that is too often overlooked as managers get intoxicated with the change and the potential outcome, or when they get driven by a deadline that becomes more important than the outcome.

Mapping out a process entails conducting a high-level review of the process flow.

Mapping out the change and reviewing the implications are the first steps in a multistep process to ensure your change hits the mark you set and actually moves the ball ahead. Mapping out a process is just that—it is a high-level review of what happens in a process flow, a flowchart of a process and its steps. Then, once you have outlined the process, you need to review that process and advise those potentially impacted of the change. Here you will trace a transaction through the new process end to end and see what potential adjustments to the operating systems and flows or to your change you need to make to ensure your execution.

If the MIS manager had reviewed his change with our head of technology, he would have found out rather quickly that the stop code could not be used without severe implications and that the downstream impacts could not be dealt with, which would have caused him to rethink using the field.

As you change things in your area, you need to have folks first tell you how the current process works and then you need to list the implications and impacted areas. That becomes your change control process and a checklist for all your changes to ensure that there are no adverse impacts down the road.

Quantifying the Changes

As you begin to manage within a system that works for and with you to execute activities that will move you closer to your vision, you will inevitably change things, often more than once. Having learned the lesson of mapping the process end to end, I am confident that you now know the value of implications associated with change, and not only will you avoid adverse impacts, but you just may eliminate unnecessary work downstream as changes are viewed more broadly. The tedious work in change is actually identifying what *exactly* is going to change. We call it *quantifying the change*. What that entails is once the general change is described, there are a series of changes typically associated with it that need be quantified and acted upon to complete the change.

Let's imagine you are going to change your route to work in the morning to avoid construction. First you would map out the new route, your personal end-to-end process map. If you carpool, you may have to adjust pickup time, a downstream implication. As you run through this new route in your mind, you would begin to quantify the change—is this a longer route? If it is, you need to change the frequency at which you buy gas and adjust your budget to accommodate the additional fuel. Are you now traveling on a toll road, where you will need exact change or a speed pass to make the route change easier to navigate? And since you are no longer passing the donut shop, what do you do for breakfast? These are all examples of quantifying the change.

In my 30+ years of managing, I cannot tell you how many times I have heard someone say, "We didn't understand all the aspects of that change," or "When we changed the process, we never figured this would happen." That is the importance of quantifying the change, but the byproduct is that people have a greater understanding of the change and can effectively execute it to the desired outcome—and don't underestimate the power of understanding.

Quantifying a change refers to identifying what exactly is going to change.

The byproduct of quantifying changes is that people gain a greater understanding of the changes so they can effectively execute them.

Testing the Change

If our MIS manager would have changed one record instead of every darn record we had (it still gets me even today!) and traced the impact, he would have seen the problem and avoided it. Testing, complete end-to-end testing. The systems gurus call it *regression testing*—testing your change to ensure it has the desired impact and that all your policies and procedures that support it are adequate. The important thing about testing is that you test for the expected result.

You should document a test case with inputs and expected outputs and then run through the test and see whether the expected outputs match the actual outputs. You need to test the change

The most important part of testing is to test for the expected result.

Complete end-to-end testing is known as regression testing.

itself, which is a *unit test*, but also everything around it; that is the regression test.

When installing a system, producing a new report, or changing a process, there is an expected outcome. I recall putting in a new process flow in an underwriting area. We created a new role called *junior underwriter*. This person would prepare the loan file to be underwritten; the theory here was that the paperwork organization, the mathematical checks, and the verification and sorting of documents took valuable time, and our highly paid, highly skilled underwriters could actually produce more files if they did not have to spend their time on these remedial tasks. The more files they produced, the faster the decisions were made, the more loans we closed, and the less opportunity for a competitor to steal away a customer as they waited for an underwriting decision.

The process was outlined and it was quantified. We understood the changes we needed to make, wrote the procedures, trained the people, and were off to the races. Oh, and everybody loved it—it was great!

At the monthly business meeting, the managers told me how great this new process was, and people really enjoyed the new workflow; it seemed to be a morale booster as well. "Wow, that's great," I thought, and then I asked the question that stunned the room. "How many more files are we underwriting as a result of the new process?" There was some silence and then the response came.

"Well, we expect to see that improve, but nothing right now." We had hired six junior underwriters, changed the job descriptions for the underwriters, re-stacked the underwriting workspace, put in new process flows, and we didn't even know if what we had done would work.

We didn't know because we didn't test it. Had we tested it, we would have learned what further process adjustments would have been required, what behaviors were critical to success, and how the current systems would need to change to support the new workflows and roles we introduced. We learned all that over the course of the next six months, because although we didn't realize it, every day we were living an uncontrolled test of our new process.

The alternative would have been to set up one workstation, have test files go through that station, and document the outcomes to see whether they matched our expected outcomes—namely, more files underwritten at the same or better quality in execution.

Training for New Behaviors

As part of any operational change you put into place, there are procedures that change, and in doing so, you expect people's behaviors to change. In essence, you are giving them a new job, because you are altering or changing their job. The key to success in any new job is training. For every change you make, if you do nothing else, make sure you train your people on the change, what behaviors they need to undertake, and which ones they can stop as a result of the change.

> For every change you make, you must train your people on the change—what behaviors they need to undertake and which ones they can stop as a result of the change.

We implemented an automated reconciliation of all our trial balance accounts in an accounting department I ran. Prior to this project, we had a person whose job it was to come in every morning at 7:30 and reconcile the report balances to ensure the department's 25 or so reports that we used to do our jobs in the course of the day balanced or matched. It took about a half hour and was about 80-percent accurate on its best day because while the totals matched, the ins and outs didn't always, which wrought havoc. The automation allowed for a line-by-line assurance that all transactions hit across all reports 100-percent verified.

The project had been completed for about five weeks and had a favorable impact, especially on the quality of our work output because we were dealing with errorless data. I came in one morning and saw our "reconciler" hard at work. As I walked by her desk, I was puzzled. She was doing the morning reconciliation—the very reconciliation we had automated. "Kathy, what are you doing here this morning?" I asked. I pretended that I actually didn't know what she was doing, but come to think of it, I really didn't!

"I am doing the morning recon." She flipped the response back to me as if I should have known.

"Why?" I asked.

She looked at me in confusion and said, "We always do the recon to ensure the balances match." I then explained to her that the automation project we completed a month ago now ensured the balances matched and that the recon wasn't needed anymore. Her response was somewhat comical; she asked, "Are you sure?"

I nodded and said, "Positive." No one had communicated to her that the recon process was no longer needed; in fact, the newly written procedure still referred to it! The new update to the department procedures still reflected the process we eliminated!

Lesson: In any change, it is important to communicate what you need to do and what you no longer need to do!

Validating

After you implement a change, audit or check the new process or change about 30 to 45 days later to see whether it works.

Simply put, inspect what you expect! After you have implemented a change, it is a good idea to audit or check the new process or change about 30 to 45 days later to see whether it took and to see whether the staff is executing not only the spirit of the change, but the letter of it as well. You will find that if you use this process, the validation will result in valuable feedback and may even give you insight into continuous improvement in change management and implementation. The validation consists of an audit to see the results and the actual compliance with the procedures and then a debriefing with the unit to discuss the results and adjustments, as well as to hear any issues and feedback on the change itself.

Like all management practices, change is a system of practices and behaviors supplemented by policy and procedures. As you repetitively go through this system, the repetition creates discipline, and culture becomes stronger and stronger. The result is an organization of continuous improvement and development through change.

So change really comes down to a mindset of understanding, capability, and internalization that is supported by a management system that underscores the operational aspects of change, namely:

1. Review the end-to-end process to identify all dependencies and downstream changes.
2. Quantify the changes.
3. Test the changes.
4. Train for the new behaviors required.
5. Validate.

As you consider the changes you will make in the next 90 days, using this methodology will not only allow the changes to take root, but will ensure that you are building a system of changes that is sustainable and allows you to have flexibility and control as your organization implements the changes it needs to bring about your vision.

Chapter 4

Communications

- Focus Groups
- Monthly Newsletter: Question-and-Answer Mailbox
- Brown-Bag Lunches
- The Town Hall
- Website Portal for Announcements, Policies and Procedures, and Important News

One of the greatest attributes any leader or manager can have is the ability to communicate well. Every aspect of what you do as a manager requires you to communicate, and while there are different styles and approaches to communications, if you are going to succeed you need to find what works for you as a manager. Not everyone communicates in the same manner, and the larger the group, the more ways you must communicate. In this context, communication is defined as message sent/message received. If you can pass that simple test, you have communicated.

As a manager, almost everything you do sends a message, and the higher up you are on the organizational chart, the more messages you send. However, even the front-line supervisor sends a message with every movement he makes in the course of the day and every word he says.

It's not only what you say, but how you say it that matters. Implementing effective communications begins with identifying the ways you will reach the population with which you want to communicate. Having mainstay vehicles teaches people to look for messages at a certain place and time and from certain people. A company website; a department share point or blog; a monthly meeting; focus groups, such as "ask the boss," "breakfast update," or "brown-bag lunch"; a monthly newsletter; and town halls are all vehicles of communication that people will go to in order to receive and to give information. They will become points of communications for your organization that people can rely on to get clarification, facts, and most importantly, feedback on what concerns them.

Earlier, we talked about management systems that feed you as the manager; a communications system will feed the organization, and it will feed them *you!* Your thoughts, ideas, progress reports, changes, and energy create the lifeblood of the organization.

Here is what a communications system may look like in an organization:

- Focus groups (one to three per month)
- Monthly newsletter with question-and-answer mailbox
- Brown-bag lunches on topics
- Monthly town halls
- Website portal for announcements, policies and procedures, and important news

These staples in an organization ensure the flow of information and define where people can go to get information. There is an additional benefit: These places become reliable sources of information and can combat the miscommunication, competitive propaganda, grapevine, and rumor mill that are all inherent in the workplace.

Focus Groups

As a manager, I absolutely love focus groups, mainly because they give you a chance to interact with people, be a role model, and set the tone for how you want your organization to run. Running effective focus groups is not an easy task by any means. To begin with, as a manager you want to create a nonthreatening environment for people to speak up, and you want a chance to react to what is being said and communicate to them in a manner that they a) understand and b) can carry forward to others.

You want to avoid fixing things from the focus group chair—a practice that I call *hero managing*, where managers use their power at the table to instantly cure an issue. It sounds great, except it undermines the leadership team that works for you, and the solutions usually are not well thought out and are often incomplete, creating more problems than the one you attempted to fix in the first place.

> As a focus group leader, be sure to create a nonthreatening environment in which people can share.

The keys to running an effective focus group are listening, understanding, acknowledging, and finally sharing your thoughts. Do not be afraid to say you do not know or understand or that you need to think about something. You are a manager, and with that title comes an expectation that you think about things to get the best solution. Focus groups aren't interviews for the job—they *are* the job!

> No hero managing! Try to avoid fixing things from the focus group chair.

My approach to focus groups is for people to weigh in on what is working and what is not working in an organization. I deliberately lead with what is working, because the things that are going correctly give a frame of reference to address the things that are not working the way you want them to. I often ask, "Why is it that XYZ works but ABC doesn't?" This forces the thought process to the core of why things work, and hopefully you can export the good to improve the not-so-good.

I was in a focus group in a customer call center one morning, and I started off with the question, "What does a good day in the call center look like?" My vision of a good day in the call center included phones lighting up, people addressing customers' concerns with a smile because they had all the solutions to customers' inquiries and issues, people moving about quickly and deliberately, a certain buzz in the place.... Even now, as I write this, I can see the place before me, and I am getting excited to be there! But the response I received stunned me.

What's working? What's not working? This is a good way to approach a focus group.

"A good day in the call center would be a day when there were no calls," was the first response I received. First I thought it was a joke; in fact, a few folks laughed sheepishly.

But then heads nodded, and a second comment verified what I heard. "Yeah, that would be great. Then we could actually get some work done, and people wouldn't be so freaky." I paused for a moment, having listened to the comments. The next step was to understand.

"Let me understand this a bit," I began. "You think a good day in a place that exists to answer customer calls is when no customer would call? Why?" They then began to tell me that they had no tools to help the customers most of the time, and that just led to further frustration on everyone's part. I asked what tools they would need, and they began to list off ideas for tools and information they needed. The odd part was that they knew where the information was; they just weren't allowed to access it. I acknowledged that we had a problem, and they clearly knew that I understood the issue.

A focus group is not a venue for you to vent your own frustrations.

In a focus group setting, most managers want to fix the issues they hear about, or they want to vent their own frustrations with their management teams for allowing such situations to occur and exist—two common mistakes you want to avoid. Remember, as the manager, people expect you to think, so do just that! As tempted as I was to promise a fix to the issue or to comment on how ludicrous the workflow was, I refrained. There is no value in managing from a focus group chair. It feeds the ego, so be careful—and remember that this is a meeting about communications, not operational design. Your test is message sent and message received—that's it.

The last piece of the focus group is the manager sharing his or her thoughts and observations. I asked the group how we might get to these types of issues in the future, rather than waiting for a focus group. They had some good thoughts, including a once-a-month meeting to discuss improvement opportunities within the department.

The focus group is a tool that gives you a forum to let people talk about their work environment in a constructive fashion, as well as about surface issues that you can deal with through your management team. Here again, whether you have 20 people or 2,000 people, the focus group tool is essential because it allows data to flow to you when it might not otherwise reach you.

In larger organizations, focus groups should be with similar levels of staff to create a common set of data among that population and so you can have meaningful dialogue within the group that is beneficial to everyone.

In a team managers' focus group recently, one of the team leads remarked that our employee time-tracking system would not allow people to put in vacation time beyond the current month. This particularly caused an issue for her because on Day 1 of a given month, she was finding out where the shortages in staffing were occurring, and often it was the same week as she was finding out. Reaction time was short, notification to people that they could not have the time off they requested was not timely, and the result was chaotic scheduling that occurred the first week of every month.

Before I could say anything by way of understanding the issue, a second team lead spoke up and told her that, in fact, was not the way the system really worked. Some of the other leads nodded accordingly—you could schedule 90 days out; you simply had to press Alt+Shift+S, and a drop-down would appear asking you how far out you wanted to go. The system defaulted to 30 days, but Alt+Shift+S was a viable workaround. The point is that sometimes focus groups are simply people talking about common issues as employees, and more often than not someone has figured out the solution. But if the environment you create as a manager isn't one that creates dialogue among its employees, you are not optimizing the knowledge because it never gets shared.

Group similar levels of staff to create focus groups in larger organizations.

It was such a revelation that many of the managers suggested we do a communication bulletin to all managers about this little-known fact. When we did, the buzz on the floor was deafening!

People were excited that they had been heard and that we "changed our policy" to allow them to schedule out three months in advance! Sometimes it amazes me what good communications can do in an organization.

The most important thing about focus groups is that you will receive many, many data points. At some point you need to connect the dots and, with your management team, change the behaviors, policies, and processes; clarify the practices; communicate; and respond. Otherwise, you are simply collecting data with no true value added.

The question is when do you respond to issues you hear in a focus group? And the answer is pretty simple: when you have heard or seen enough occurrences that you know there is a response required. How do you respond is the next logical question, and the approach should be to engage the management team and the management process in a response and credit the focus group process, so that people know focus groups are a valuable tool for them to resolve conflicts, protect good practices, and export ideas.

You shouldn't be the only one who has focus groups. If you manage managers, then they need to have focus groups as well. You should discuss the feedback and actions surrounding the focus groups across the organization so it becomes a constructive dialogue with the employees and the management team.

It's important that no one ever gets promoted and no one ever gets fired for a comment made in a focus group—the expectation is open communications in a free environment.

Never promote or fire anyone for a comment made in a focus group! Remember, it's supposed to be a safe environment for sharing.

Also, the expectation of what will be done with the information is critical. You should avoid conclusions and managing from the pulpit in a focus group, but where there are nonnegotiable behaviors, you need to state that, too. So in a town hall or a focus group, if someone is not respectful of others and respect is a value you hold, then call them on it. If someone is absolutely wrong about something and it can cause issues, address it right there. I was in a town hall setting, and a woman stood up and said that she had heard we were not giving out pay raises to employees so that management could get bigger pay raises. I responded the same way you probably reacted to this absurd rumor. I simply said, "What good would that do, and how is that consistent with our values as an organization?" People nodded in approval, and some even applauded.

I was in a focus group, and the topic of reimbursement for gas mileage came up. It seems with rising gas prices, people wanted to increase the amount that we reimbursed them for mileage. Now, that practice is governed by the IRS, and any amount paid over that would be taxable income. It is also fairly consistent among all employers. When that issue was raised, I explained the position and stated that we would not be changing it, and I gave them the rationale as to why. That closed the issue. There are rare times in a focus group when you can do just that and end the buzz right there.

People who participate in focus groups need to carry the message out from the focus group to the population so everyone benefits from the interaction. You can (and should) publish on your web-page or communication vehicle the key topics of discussion and perhaps resolutions that came from focus groups to allow people again to see the value and catch the wave of information.

In larger organizations, there should be a steady focus group schedule that is centrally managed and data collected for the management team to act on. This allows all the senior managers to get to know employees and employees to know and interact with management. It also serves to break down the barrier to communication—the natural "rank wall" that often exists. This breakdown sets the tone for an open and interactive dialogue between employees and management.

Here again, the more you interact, the greater the temptation to start to manage from the focus group chair. *Do not do it!* The rule is to manage through your structure. Also, the temptation is to promote, fire, and judge from that focus group chair—here again, that is management suicide.

I was a participant in a focus group with a senior manager once, and he began to engage with one of the team members on a few topics. The team member was very articulate, opinionated, and presented herself well. At one point, the manager actually said, "You have excellent thoughts. I have an opening for a chief of staff, and I want you to come and see me Monday to talk about that role." She was by far the worst performer in our group. She did get the job and wound up fired a few months into the role, but the damage was greater than that. The reputation and credibility of that senior manager was questioned over and over again after that episode. He lost the respect of his peers as the story ran rapidly through the organization. There was nothing immoral about his behavior; he just made a bad judgment call. But the rumor mill and the poor performance of the woman both before and after the job exposed him to undue criticism

The judgment error was making a hiring decision in a focus group setting, rather than following the human resources posting process that he, as a senior leader, was supposed to support. And finally, he made a bad hiring decision on top of it all. That is what can happen when you abuse a powerful tool like a focus group. Remember the purpose of a focus group. It's simple: Obtain data points from which to understand the overall environment you are managing. That and that alone is the single purpose of a focus group. Anything else you may want to attempt to do is a misuse of focus groups and can only have a negative impact.

Focus groups should be informal; they should allow people to voice their opinions, concerns, and also accomplishments and positives. That is why my favorite focus group—and frankly, the only one I subscribe to—is the "what's working and what's not working" focus group. Here, participants list and talk about the things that are going well and the things that are not going well in the company and in the department.

Focus groups should be informal; they are not meant to emulate formal staff meetings.

This type of focus group features questions such as: How would you improve that? Why do you think that goes so well? Has it always been that way? What did it look like when it worked well? What would it look like if it worked well? Avoid talking about a particular person or manager or reacting specifically if that should come up. Move off the topics once you understand the core issue and you articulate the core issue so people know you understand it. Sometimes you have to move off the topic when you don't fully get it. Tell the team that and then come back to it or follow up through your managers or human resources team.

Take notes. You will have many focus groups, and you will want to look at your notes for trends, great ideas that came up, and follow-up issues. And, you'll want to read them over again from time to time to help you relate and take action. I always read my focus group notes before I do a town hall or departmental meeting or have a review with my managers; it sharpens my delivery, awareness, and understanding.

Monthly Newsletter: Question-and-Answer Mailbox

A great tool to foster communications is a monthly letter to the organization or to your entire manager population that describes your progress toward the departmental goals with the appropriate metrics, comparisons, and trends. This also is an excellent place to address relevant topics, from market conditions to the new copiers that are being installed throughout the organization. It is a great venue for communicating. In addition, with today's technology, you can distribute extremely efficiently and use an electronic receipt to ensure that all the employees have seen it and have it for reference. You can store the newsletters in a common drive or provide a link on your website. Managers can review them at their staff meetings and give you feedback. In addition, these days many executives have a management communication blog, where they address daily issues, markets, competition, and strategies.

In some cases, mailing a hard copy of the newsletter to employees' homes brings in the employee's support system outside of work and serves as a recruiting tool and an information source.

I remember having sent such a mailing to all employees' homes, and we did a feature spot on our benefits. I received a personal letter not too long after we sent that out from the wife of one of our employees, who thanked me for sending the letter. It seems her husband didn't understand that we had eye-care benefits, and not only did he never sign up for them, but he had four children who all wore glasses or contacts. Our plan covered the annual eye checkup and had discounts available for certain lenses, frames, and contacts. She estimated that she would save $446 per year as a result, and she signed her letter with, "What a great place you have there, Mr. Meola."

Also, sending that type of communication home has the employee reading it in a different setting, typically with more thought and reflection.

I would only caution you that those types of publications often wind up in the competition's hands, in the hands of regulators, and in the good old *Wall Street Journal*, so you want to be sure you have the broader audience in mind when you send them. If you

Monthly newsletters can be distributed electronically or via snail-mail in hard copy.

think I am kidding, feel free to Google some of my memos—you will find them out there!

That is not to say you shouldn't use these tools, but rather that you should make sure you have your compliance team or legal team give you some guiding principles or even review them before you send them.

Newsletters need to communicate valuable information and do so in a way that people will want to read them. They can contain illustrations, charts, and so on—maybe even a cartoon or a very informal tone in a particular section. Depending on the resources you have available, your newsletter could really take off into a communication masterpiece. But never make the mistake of having someone else write your message for you. You can delegate the formats, charts, and numbers, but when you are going to write a monthly letter or blog, then *you* should write your section.

When writing a blog communication, be careful to keep the topics general. Blogs should create dialogue, conversations, and focus in the workplace. They should not get very specific, and they should not go on endlessly about a particular topic.

Whether you write an email letter, a blog, or snail mail to create dialogue in an organization, most managers and employees need a place to ask questions and get answers.

Clarity is a key ingredient in any communications strategy for a manager. Clarity is an amazing thing—when any team has it on any subject or topic, the results will be better, guaranteed.

Think about a football team in which each member breaks the huddle, but not all understand exactly what the play and the formation called in the huddle were. What are the chances of success? Ever see a quarterback scramble and point to the direction in which he will throw the ball? That is proof that clarity is better than the alternative, even when you are telling your team and the opponent at the same time!

Newsletters are not about you, but they are a way to let people know what you are thinking as the leader—and what they want to know is how what you are thinking will affect them! Sometimes an employee-run newsletter with you writing a paragraph or two in a section is better received—mixed in with what employees think employees want to know would be a message from you. It is a valuable tool because if the employee team running the letter connects with the organization, they typically do so on a much better level than a communications department or writers do, because they are living the issues every day. Your placement of a message in such a letter will emphasize certain things in a setting that is very real to people, and in my experience will be read as such.

Brown-Bag Lunches

Brown-bag lunches are meetings held at lunchtime where employees come to a specific area to have their lunch and obtain information or receive training on a topic. That is the key—training or information. Anything beyond that is simply not a good use of the forum. This isn't a place for exchanges of information, problem solving, or discussion—those are more for focus-group settings or specific meetings to solve problems.

Brown-bag lunches are not a place for discussion or problem solving. They are training tools.

Brown-bag lunches are great places to discuss employee benefits, the new building construction, the upcoming facilities move, the new overtime system, and things that require a transfer of information. They are good places to discuss and present best practices in management and how-to topics ranging from user applications and Word or Excel training to how to be a better manager!

This is a real opportunity to coach the masses on particular aspects of managing people and giving presentations. And it is absolutely a great venue for young managers to learn how to present through on-the-job training by letting them present.

Let a young manager present at a brown-bag lunch— it's a great place for him or her to test the waters.

Brown-bag lunches should be aimed as distribution vehicles for your message, tools, concepts, and information. They also are excellent for simply showcasing employees and best practices. They are a critical part of a good communication plan in any organization.

One of my favorite brown-bag stories centers around a lunch program we did that simply explained the organizational chart and what departments did what in the organization. This information was presented by each supervisor. The brown bags were extremely well attended, and we had to add on 10 to 12 more than we scheduled because people were literally getting in line for them.

After we completed the sessions, an employee who had started with us about a year earlier posted for a role in our help-desk area.

She actually had been a help supervisor in her previous company, but she was laid off as a result of that company outsourcing the help desk. She had assumed that our help desk was also outsourced and thus took a role in our customer service center as a team lead.

Not only did she get the job in the help-desk area, but she brought enthusiasm, technical competence, and ideas for improvement to an area that sorely needed it. She was promoted to the manager role after only eight months in the supervisor position and was equally successful.

In an ironic twist, I learned about all of this at, yes, a brown-bag lunch—the topic that day was "stories of success in the organization."

The lesson here continues to be the importance of communication and the understanding that no one venue can do it all for a manager—you must have a plan with several avenues of communication for employees to drive down to get to the end goal, which is knowledge.

The Town Hall

One of the most powerful venues—and my personal favorite venue—is the infamous town hall. You have seen them on TV, used by presidential candidates, famous people, and all types of executives. The format of a town hall has gradually become less and less formal, and they are best when there is engagement with the audience—a.k.a. the town!

Dialogue is the key in a town hall—they're for discussion, not speech-making.

The key to a town hall is engagement. Many managers confuse a town hall with a speech that has a question-and-answer segment, but there is a big difference. In a town hall, you may want to warm up with a 20- or even 30-minute message, but that message must be around topics that will engage your audience. In contrast, in a speech you may want to give the audience information, some of which may elicit a response, but not all. In a town hall, your remarks must spur the engagement of your audience. You want a dialogue around the topics people want to talk about.

The best way to formulate engaging topics is to find out what people want you to talk about. An email, a website box, or any method you choose to gather the topics (not the questions) that people want to hear about is the best way to ensure that their interest will be engaged and kept and that a dialogue is sure to occur.

The environment of the town hall is the second key to ensuring that there will be dialogue and engagement. It should be well-lit, with some energetic music, and sometimes some light snacks, such as candy bars, popcorn, ice cream bars, and water.

Make sure the seating is such that all people can see the speaker and that he or she can see them as well.

Provide an informal, relaxed atmosphere for a town hall.

You should start the town hall by letting the audience know what the topics will be, and also letting them know that they are there to participate. As you present the topics and discuss them as a speaker, pause and tell the audience that you want to hear what they have to say about a certain topic, or tell them what you *need* to hear from them on a topic.

Your speech in this setting should leave something on the table to spur dialogue. Your goal is to engage them.

Let me give you an example. Let's imagine you are going to speak to the group on the financial performance of the organization. In a speech that will be followed by questions and answers, the speech would be about the financials—what they are and what that means—and you would walk through a few slides (all financial in nature) with a few charts, graphs, and tables telling the audience how the company performed financially for the time period. You would also make some comments on how the financials actually work by explaining some terms and so on. The questions would most likely be along the technical lines. A question might be something like, "You said our expense ratio was better than we planned by 6 percent. What drives that?" This is an example of how your speaking controls the questions. If you talk technical, then expect technical questions, because that is who you are relating to—in other words, technical in and technical out.

If it were a town hall, your presentation would be about the employees and their actions and then would end with the result of the expenses or any topic you are discussing. It might look like this:

"Expenses: 6 percent improvement! We reduced overtime in shipping as a result of introducing part-time positions that better matched the workload. We continue to look for opportunities to better match staffing to workload in all departments." As you read this, what is the first thing you think about? Are they going to do this in my department? What will be the impact on me? Will I earn less money, get laid off...what's going on here? Engagement in, engagement out! See the difference?

In the question-and–answer session that follows that line of comments, people will talk about workloads, they will talk about staffing, and they will tell you their concerns—all data points you need to be more effective in your management of expenses related to labor.

Town halls are all about audience engagement—get them involved!

In a speech, you typically do not engage the audience until the specified time, whereas in a town hall you can engage them after each topic is put out there or even while you are putting it out there: "I would like to talk about workloads. Our goal is to match the activity with the staffing. Who has an example where we are doing that well? Who has an example where we are not doing that so well? Who has an idea how we might do that better? What do you think of that idea for your department? What would be the challenges in doing that in your area?"

If you are comfortable, it's a good idea in town halls to walk around, as it keeps the energy and attention span up in the room. It's also a good idea to tell a story versus giving a speech on any of the topics.

This is not a new concept. All the great philosophers of their time told stories to make a point, parables that gave examples that people could remember, and that is the key point—people remember, and they learn. Stories grab people's attention and hold it—provided they are interesting, of course. People repeat stories, but I have yet to hear someone repeat a speech!

Finally, as with any speech or presentation, *prepare!* Think to yourself about what might come up and how you want to address it. What points do you want to make, and where do you want to have some discussion? Remember, this town hall is as much for you as it is for the audience—communication is about a two-way street called *dialogue.*

Website Portal for Announcements, Policies and Procedures, and Important News

Knowing where to go for information is as important as the information itself. In every organization there needs to be a "source"—a reliable place where people can find out about policies, procedures, and changes. It needs to be a place for people to get information at their own pace and on their own so they can read and absorb it at their rate of intake, and they can also ask questions to get clarity or understanding. This is one of the most important things a company, organization, department, or even a desk can have.

In today's world, technology allows us to use websites, portals, and share points at the lowest levels of an organization for unbelievably inexpensive costs with truly incredible benefits.

Now the sites are also interactive and can provide web-based training embedded in the procedures, Q&A formats, frequently asked questions, and even demos and tests for the reader.

Each morning, when every employee must log on to the system for anything from email to a production system, you have an opportunity to communicate to all your people, even if there are a million of them!

A portal is a useful tool. It is a splash page from which people can navigate. Yahoo!, AOL, Hotmail, and the like all have you log on to their central page, where they have information waiting for you. You can do the same for your employees every day. This is a very effective way to establish a culture, communicate with people, align the organization as to what is important and what your goals are, as well as help your employees through the day.

Many companies have a central site that employees can go to, but few companies have employees log onto that site to navigate to anything they need—and that's a major difference. It is not as cumbersome as it appears. Employees log on, with all their tools and systems a click away, and the page appears with a message. It could be commentary on daily market events, coupled with upcoming important events or information, a video presentation, change alerts, and so on—all geared toward making people more informed.

Communications is all about information and getting that information out to all different people. So it follows that there is no single communication magic wand, but rather a plan that has several branches, all tied together with common, aligned, and supportive messages. In addition, at the cornerstone of communications is clarity, and clarity requires dialogue. The trick here is message sent and message received—constantly test your message to see if and how it landed, and address it over and over again until it's clear. The only way to perfect communications is to engage people in the processing of information, and here again, the more methods you can effectively manage and keep tied together, the better off you will be. Don't overdo it, though. Remember, you need a plan that is effective and ties everything together. Three or four avenues well run and well executed will get the communication process rolling even in the largest organizations. Repetition breeds familiarity, and that breeds confidence.

Chapter 5

The Management Process

- The Importance of a Management Process
- Implementing a Management Process
- Ensuring Success with Management Processes
- Understanding Frequency and Depth
- Using Committees

Every manager needs to establish a management process in order to be successful. A *management process* is a combination of repeatable, sustainable activities fueled by data points that enable the manager and the unit to execute the objective or the mission, which in turn allows them to achieve the vision. See Figure 5.1.

Figure 5.1
The management process.

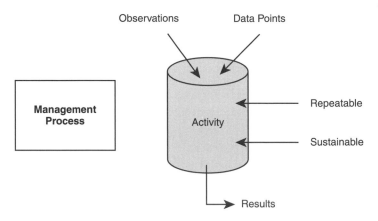

The Importance of a Management Process

All people have a routine they follow in everyday life that allows them to maximize their own individual happiness and success. Some people exercise every morning, drink a glass of orange juice, have a bowl of oatmeal, and read the paper, and they are ready to take on the world and what it has to offer for the day. If that routine gets disturbed, then they are off kilter for the day. So it is with a management process.

When I was a young manager in the finance department of a Fortune 100 company, one of the many responsibilities I had was to produce the monthly financial management report. This report included an analysis of our profit and loss statement and the key drivers of that statement, and it took about seven days for us to produce it. In my first three months on the job, I learned the value of a management process.

My boss would call me about a day or two after the close and ask me when the report would be ready. I would tell him we were in process, and he would then start to ask me questions, as if the report was completed. I would write them down and go out to my department and start to rifle through reports and piece together the answers, disrupting the entire workflow as I went, which ultimately made the reports late because we were working on the questions instead of the report. Of course, because it was a work in progress, sometimes we would get the wrong answer or an incomplete answer. Other times our numbers would not reconcile to reports we issued as part of the accounting close because we issued reports before we were ready to issue them. The deadline for the report would come, and we were not yet to the part of the process where we would tic and tie out all the numbers.

It was chaos at its best each month for about three or four months. It finally occurred to me why my manager would call me prior to the report being issued and start with the questions—he simply did not know when the report would be done each month. There was no way for him to know when the report would be issued, so he asked as he began to wonder about the monthly financial results. Finally, I realized the solution. I plotted out the steps for doing the report and then looked at a calendar and sent him a note with the day when the report would be ready for him each month.

His initial response was that he couldn't wait for the report to be issued to get some of his answers because his boss was curious about the results analysis as well. That led us to a "flash report," in which we simply did a few of the sections first—unreconciled and broad explanations that were for the most part directionally correct. We organized who did what a bit differently in the department so we could produce the flash each month on the second workday, followed by a flash update on the fourth and the final report on the seventh. An amazing thing happened! We stopped getting the panicked phone calls, I stopped running around the department disrupting everyone, and my boss thought I was a genius because he now received information five days before he began getting questioned by his superiors.

What had happened here? I had created a repeatable, sustainable set of activities fueled by data points that created an end result that achieved our goal. I had created a management process.

> Management processes are created by identifying repeatable, sustainable activities driven by data points.

Each day, that little finance department knew where we stood in producing the monthly financial report, and we knew what we had to do each day to achieve success. The recipient of our process's work product, the boss, knew what to expect (and when) every step of the way. He in turn planned his update meeting so he had the information in advance and was able to update his boss with the information on a timely basis.

Process maps will help you create and adjust workflow.

I expanded this practice further and began to plot everything we did and put it on the calendar (see Figure 5.2). I later came to understand that these plots had a name; they were called *process maps*. Putting these process maps on the calendar created a workflow for the organization, with interim steps that I, as a manager, could measure and monitor along the way. I could make adjustments when I needed to and change staffing to ensure we were adequately positioned to meet our delivery dates. Each morning we would meet as a unit and look at the calendar, and we would ask ourselves whether we met the previous day's goal and whether we could achieve the current day's goal. Depending upon the answer, we made adjustments. That was a management process!

Figure 5.2

Putting process maps on the calendar creates a workflow that can be measured and monitored.

Work Calendar

1	2	3	4	5	6
Begin Report Production		Review Data Balance to G/L			
7	8	9	10	11	12
Review Report Internally			Review Report with Boss		
13	14	15	16	17	18
	Make Report Adjustments			Issue Final Report	
19	20	21	22	23	24
			Debrief Report Process for Improvement		

Soon we began to think in terms of the management process. We looked for ways to cut out time in the process, to improve the execution, to eliminate steps, to increase the quality of what we did—all because we were in touch with the steps of what we did and we had a process to measure, monitor, and manage the process.

Implementing a Management Process

Whether you manage divisions, departments, units, teams, or even your own desk, you need to do so with a management process. To begin with, you need to ask yourself what the key drivers of results in your area of responsibility are and how you would measure them. To answer that, you often need to see the process map of the activities that achieve results. You then need to measure the activities in a meaningful way to see whether you are progressing toward your goal at the required pace. You need to do this every day, and you need to do it at the appropriate level that coincides with your responsibilities and accountability. My boss in that little finance department looked at a flash report on the second day of the month to see where he stood in the financial results. It gave him the ability to affect those results; because we closed the books on the fifth day, he could book more sales, increase his reserves, and accelerate payments to obtain further discounts.

Ask yourself how you can measure the key drivers of results in your area?

For my boss to receive that flash on Day 2, I had to monitor the steps to get there for about nine days prior to ensure that the data was good. He didn't need to do that because I did—in fact, he couldn't possibly do that because he had a dozen financial departments to manage!

Ultimately, I was accountable and responsible for ensuring the issuance of timely and accurate reports, and he needed to make certain that the explanations of the activity made sense and were actionable. That is why he quizzed the results and we produced the responses. We would also quiz the results to ensure they had integrity and were balanced and reconciled at a much more detailed level.

Using Measurements and Metrics

Measurements or metrics are the key to running a great operation. What you measure you will understand, and what you understand you will be able to manage. It is key to measure the right set of activities that is consistent with the result you are trying to achieve.

I managed a loan processing organization for one of the country's top lenders in the '90s. Our goal at the time was to close a loan in 30 days. When I took over the department, the sales force was constantly complaining that the competition was better than we were at closing loans, and in fact we were too slow. My operations team would contend that we were fine, and in fact we had reports that demonstrated that, on average, we closed loans in 28 days! As the new manager of the area, I was stumped. I was told that the sales team always complained that we were not good enough, when in fact the stats spoke for themselves—or did they?

I asked to see the raw data that made up the 28-day calculation. Honestly, being an accountant at heart, I was looking for an error in the calculation. What I found was even more astounding than that. When you measure a result versus the activity that makes up the result, you have to wait for the completion of the cycle to see the result. I discovered that while we *averaged* 28 days to close a loan, we had literally hundreds of loans over 28 days that, when they closed, would drive the averages upward to about 47 days. But as long as they remained open or in process, they would never be in the closed-loan report. I also discovered something that has remained with me throughout my entire management career—the law of averages according to Meola!

Here is how that works: We began to measure the days in process versus the closed loans, and we further began to age the days in process in increments of five days, so 0–5, 6–10, 11–15, 16–20, and so on (see Figure 5.3). We began to review each bucket each day and make decisions based on the data we saw. Every morning we reviewed the "bucket report" and moved loans through that process. We began to trend reasons why loans were falling into these buckets, and what we found was even more amazing. Certain product types required longer processing times because they needed more underwriting review and documentation gathering—they always took 20 to 35 days to close, even on their best day. Interestingly enough, we charged a processing fee, and yes, it was the same no matter what the product was. Soon we began to charge a lesser fee for the easier loans and a greater fee for the loans that required more activity. We then separated out the harder loans at the point when we received all loans, and we put them in a different process flow—one that was handled by our more skilled employees with lower case loads that allowed for greater processing speeds.

Figure 5.3

Department inventory MRI.

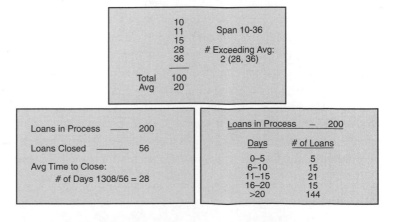

If we had two loans in the department, and one closed in 5 days and the other closed in 45 days, we "averaged" 30 days! In other words, we met our goal to average 30 days. That's like saying if you have one foot in a bucket of ice and another on a bed of hot coals, on average you are doing just fine!

It gets worse. We paid the teams that processed these loans a bonus when they met or exceeded their goals each month—the goal was to average 30 days. The easier loans were closed quickly; the harder loans that required more work were often put aside in order to close the loans that did not require much more work. As long as the late loans didn't close, the averages looked better and better as the early closes took place.

Now for the real kicker! When clients or customers withdrew their loans and went to a competitor because they were tired of waiting for us to close the loan, we called that a withdrawal or cancellation, and since those type of loans never closed—you guessed it!—they never were part of the calculation.

We also began to slice the data more, first by salesperson, and we found that some sales-team members consistently took more time to process the exact same loan than others, mainly due to insufficient or inaccurate application data. This allowed us to train the sales teams to expedite their process speeds by submitting the loans correctly and completely. Every day, we began by looking at a metric report, making operating decisions, and picking out data points to analyze to better understand the activity. Within a few months, we were closing all loans within 28 days, and we averaged 19 days to close, with a best-to-worst span of 5 to 21 days.

We changed the compensation plan to a loan-by-loan plan; we paid an incentive on any loan that closed before 28 days and a team bonus to the operating center if the days in process were less than 28. We also saw something interesting: Our cancellations and withdrawals dramatically decreased, mainly because our customers were no longer going over to our competition to get their loans closed.

All of this came out of having a management process to understand, monitor, govern, and respond to the data inflows of the business activity. It also allowed us to do something else—be proactive. The reengineering of process flows by product and charging fees that varied by product were leading industry best practices, all derived from being engaged in the business activity, which is what a management process allows you to do.

Use your management process to be proactive.

The key to a management process is inherent in its name—it is a process. The first and most important aspect is information. Too often we spend an inordinate amount of time trying to think of what the management information we would need is, then we need to build it, then we need to perfect it. By time you build this monstrosity of reporting, you are lucky if you are still in business or that you haven't been fired.

Fine-Tuning the Management Process

Allow your management process to grow by engaging and managing your team.

Data, information, and reporting are an iterative process. Even if you need to begin with a pad and pencil to measure, do so. Then daily, as you engage with and manage with your team, you will perfect the daily information, and the management process will grow out of it. You don't need a report on everything, but over time you will come to know what reports you need and what venues you need to review them. Each day you will perfect your process.

In January of 2008, I took over a company where they had a president, staff, and a process to manage. Rather than change everything to "my way" on day one, I decided that I would simply participate in the existing process and see whether it met the standards of a management process I was used to. I met with the leader one on one (at his request) each morning. During our first session, there wasn't a report or a piece of paper to be found in the meeting room. We sat there with our coffee, and he began to tell me about the business. When I asked a question, he would say, "We are doing XYZ, and we are on track." I would say, "How do you know that?" and the response would range from "I have trust and confidence in my people," to "I don't know for a fact, but I would be shocked if it weren't true," to "We talk about it at my staff meetings."

I would ask to see an existing report that would show me the trend or a measurement of the topic we had discussed, and I could see the struggle and the transformation beginning. In a few short weeks, others began to join us, mainly because we had too many follow-ups from our morning sessions. The story was the same—people simply didn't know how they knew things were running smoothly. They used phrases such as, "Audit would fail us," "Customers would be complaining," or "We would be losing money" to justify how they knew things were on track.

I asked them, "Wouldn't you want to know any of that well beforehand?" I used the analogy of going to the doctor for a regular visit—wouldn't you want to know if you were overweight, your cholesterol was high, or your heart was working too hard? Wouldn't you want to know the steps you need to take to prevent death? Or would you simply want to be carried in on a stretcher after having a massive heart attack?

That is the difference between having a management process that works for you (and with you) daily to perfect the way you manage the business and letting the business manage you.

> Don't let the business manage you! Let your management process work for you, not vice versa.

After about six months, we had daily, weekly, and monthly management information reports, scheduled meetings at specific times and places to review these reports, and action steps coming out of every meeting with positive confirmation in the form of self audits. We began to inspect what we expected to happen and make the changes we needed to ensure performance. We also recognized people, processes, and technologies that actually were performing well and exported those to areas that were not, and we saw immediate improvement.

Ensuring Success with Management Processes

Sometimes managers will balk at a management process because it gets in the way of managing the day-to-day business. This is a fatal flaw in any manager's behavior and tells you something about the manager—mainly, he or she is not ready to be a manager. Managing without a process is like flying a plane without radar: It can be done and will work better the smaller the plane is, but every once in a while you will hit a mountain, and the smaller your plane, the greater your chance of fatality.

> The larger the organization, the more important process becomes to managing.

A second key ingredient of success in a management process is defining the depth and points of engagement in the process, depending on the scope of each participant. Remember that finance department I ran and the reporting dilemma I encountered? Let me share some more of that experience to make the point of engagement and the depth points come to life for you.

The first time my boss called me and asked me whether the report was ready, you will recall that it wasn't, and he began to ask me questions. At that point my boss became the reviewer, not the reader of that report or the user. He jumped in the process head-first and inadvertently became one of us! I then became a doer or an analyst in the process, looking for raw material to respond, not focusing on the quality of the responses but rather on the responses themselves. My analysts literally became clerks, putting data together at a pace at which they could not even read or understand it. And the clerks...well, they remained clerks, but suddenly they had a bunch of other clerks running around interfering with their workload.

The wrong points of engagement and the incorrect depth of engagement rarely produce the desired results in process and further serve to destroy the process and its safety checks that are built in for quality.

Communication is key! Make sure that the entire organization is clear on the management process.

It was only when we established a process map or flow and communicated it that my boss, my employees, and I were all on the same page as to when to engage and at what level of depth.

My boss needed to know that we would have the report ready on the second day, so the first day and the preceding days he would gather other data points and views of the business and develop questions he anticipated the report would answer or shed some light on. On day two he was ready to add value with questions and extract value with new facts. I was monitoring the progress each day in the preceding days of the second workday, looking at pages as they were completed, seeing the financial story of the month develop, and deepening the analytics based on the numbers and what they told me. My analysts were busy analyzing, anticipating questions, looking for trends, and balancing the information back to the general ledger and detail journal to ensure the integrity and accuracy of the report. The clerks were gathering data, ticking and tying, formatting, graphing, and putting the report together.

Each day, I would look at where we were supposed to be versus where we were. At one point on the first workday, we had the schedule on an hour-by-hour basis—what pages were supposed to be completed by what times to really manage the conclusion of our cycle to the minute. This avoided confusion, helped me guide the staff, and helped me plan attendance, overtime, and department activity.

The minute my boss inadvertently assumed my role and started to ask questions in the pre–final report stages, he was unfamiliar with the territory and began to cause chaos. I remember he called me furious one morning, prior to us establishing the process, and said, "Tony, the report you sent me yesterday doesn't match the one you sent the day before. What the hell is going on?" Not realizing who I was talking to and what was happening, I simply said, "Of course it doesn't tie out. It never does on the second pass; we probably won't get this all reconciled for another day or so." He was beside himself: "I expect that when I see a report from your area, I do not have to check and see whether it matches the general ledger. You are a finance department, for God's sake!"

I was shocked. Didn't he know our process? No one had balanced numbers prior to the first workday in the whole company—no one. What was he talking about? Well, he was no longer the finance manager; he had dropped down to the finance reporting supervisor job, and at that level we deal with information in different forms—forms that were not ready to be engaged by the finance manager, who only dealt with finished data.

You certainly may need to engage a process before its due dates or specified times, but you need to be aware of the landscape at that time and understand what the differences are at that level of engagement. The higher up you go, the tougher it is to determine when to engage or drop in on a process, but always stay mindful of where you are on the organizational chart—and where you and your people are in the process.

If you ran a shipping department, you might want to know daily what you received to ship and what you shipped. But upon further thought, you might also, having read this book, know that as the first-line supervisor, that wouldn't be enough. If your goal was to ship all your goods within four days of receipt in the department, you now hopefully know you need to measure the activity in between.

After all, if you receive 10 items and you ship five the first day, and the second day you receive five and ship five, do you think you met your goal? It really depends on which five you ship, doesn't it? If the second five you shipped were the ones you received the second day, then you still have the original five from day one, and I would say you have a ways to go, don't you? Now, as the manager of 10 areas, one of which is shipping, maybe all you need to know is how many goods you receive and ship daily. Perhaps you know your first-line manager measures activity, so the numbers or indicators you see may be limited to those few high-level ones, and only the first-line manager needs to see the details of the activity.

As the manager of 10 areas, you are probably more focused on trending the activities of all your areas—especially where they intersect—to ensure that you can deliver all 10 departments' goals at once, whereas the individual departments are focused on their processes and activities, governing and monitoring them to maximize the results. It's the difference between managing horizontally and vertically.

In your management process, things arrive in your department, you handle them, and they leave.

The best way to start thinking about a management process is to simply think of an inventory report. Each day things come into your department, you handle them, and then they leave your department. Start with that concept and begin to track the beginning, new entry, handle, exit, and ending balance.

Trend each one across time and then begin to talk through the numbers every day. Let's take a look at what that might look like in Table 5.1.

Table 5.1 Tracking Trends

			Day				
	1	2	3	4	5	6	7
Beginning	0	5	15	10			
New Entry	5	10	5	4			
Handle	5	15	20	15			
Exit	0	0	10	0			
Ending Balance	5	15	10	15			

Suppose you are the first-line supervisor here, and Table 5.1 represents what the daily management information looks like. You look at this sample activity tracking every day. Let's look at the end of Day 2. Your inventory has tripled in two days—do you know why? Well, you are not exiting anything from the process, so that might be where you would look first. Perhaps you find out that the process takes about three days to complete. If that's true, you can predict when you will complete your inventory, and that can become a key stat for you to measure your productivity—expected ending balance.

Look at the chart again. After three days, what would you conclude about your productivity—good or bad?

Now look at the chart again. You received five pieces on Day 1. That means on Day 3, you can expect to see five pieces exit. When you look at Day 3, you see 10 pieces exit—how is that possible? Well, you received 10 pieces on Day 2, so you must have completed five of those in one day!

Feeling good? There are more data points on their way. Look at Day 4—how many should you exit? How many did you? There is definitely a problem here. You are now seeing the value of a management process. You have established data and you are reviewing it each day at a predetermined time to understand and respond to the activity. In other words, you are engaged in a combination of repeatable, sustainable activities fueled by data points that enable you and the unit to execute the objective.

Review your data each day to understand and respond to the activity.

Where you go from here is endless—you can begin to drive any activity based on the metric you establish and manage to and the frequency and depth at which you choose to operate.

Understanding Frequency and Depth

Because they are so important to a manager, we should spend a few more minutes on frequency and depth. *Frequency* is how often you will meet on a topic, and *depth* measures how much detail you will go into. Each of these sets the tone for your unit or organization in terms of what they are expected to know about their business. Each of these requires some thought because together these two aspects of a management process dial the pace of an organization and create certain behaviors.

Frequency and depth set the tone for your unit or organization.

Because these two variables are dependent, you cannot examine them alone; rather, you need to consider them together because one drives the other.

In the early '90s, the financial industry was reengineering the mortgage process. After the boom period of 1986 to 1989, the industry needed to change the way a mortgage was created. Suddenly, the product became one that was manufactured at a high rate of velocity, and speed became a competitive advantage. At the time, I was part of a team that had just come together through consolidation with one of the major commercial banks in the U.S. We met every Monday for four hours to develop, implement, and manage a new process in producing mortgages.

Every Monday we were expected to come to the meeting with all of our deliverables met, any issues we may have encountered ready to discuss, and a report on how the implementation was going in the market. It was made clear at the very first meeting that the only place (and I mean *only*) where we would engage in discussion on these topics was at this meeting. This ensured that all constituents were in on any decision- or policy-making discussion, and it also allowed time for the process and/or a recommendation to incubate for a few days before a discussion took place. In addition, it created a place for issues and problems to go in the organization every week. It allowed the organization to run, knowing that any problem would be at least discussed and often solved within seven days, and it allowed for more focus on the day-to-day business because there was a place for the distractions to go.

Your department will run better if you establish a cadence in the organization.

That is a key lesson in a management process: If you establish a cadence in an organization and a place where problems can go to be resolved you generally will find that the department runs better and free of conflicts and issues that often poison a department's success. Issues tend to grow bigger and reproduce offspring if they are not addressed immediately.

In this case, the meeting was once a week (that was the frequency) and covered every detail of our business process (that was the depth). Often it would go beyond the allotted four hours—so often that we changed the protocol of the meeting to speed the interactions and decisions several times, until the team developed a way to conduct the meeting successfully in the four-hour time period.

It was amazing—the entire organization began to revolve around the meeting. People would write recommendations to the representatives who attended the meeting on how to improve the process or change the implementation so the representative could then bring the recommendation forward and get a decision. The meeting was known for its decision-making and policy-making capabilities, and we moved an entire organization forward to a new process and way of business each Monday during the four hours we spent together, working through the issues. There was no other place that process decisions were made—none—and there was no other place that policy decisions were made. It was clear to the organization that this was the place for all policies and decisions related to processing, and they accepted that for one reason and one reason only—it was effective.

The reason this process was effective was that it had the balance of frequency and depth (see Figure 5.4). Meeting once a week for these types of decisions and discussions gave all participants a week to prepare. I don't mean study the material, I mean live the business. We were able to gather data points and inputs, visit the field, and test and see the practices, policies, and decisions we made in action. That allowed us sufficient time to gain knowledge and understanding upon which to build. At the meeting itself, there was sufficient time for discussion and debate of issues, and a protocol existed for decisions to be made. More important, a process existed for communicating the results of that meeting. Each week after the meeting, we were given 24 hours before a memo would go out to the entire organization about the meeting and the policies and decisions made, and that would be followed up by a policy and procedure bulletin with a timeline for implementation.

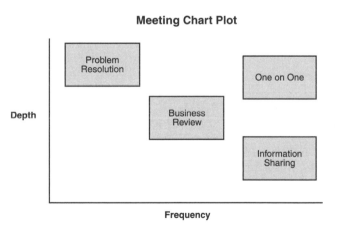

Meeting Chart Plot

Figure 5.4
The meeting balances frequency and depth.

That established the rhythm or cadence in the organization. It was very orderly and very methodical in nature, and that was how the organization ran—all as a result of the management process.

As a front-line manager in a high-volume area—or even a higher-level manager in an area going through problems—the more frequently you meet, the more momentum you establish for changed behavior. Each time I took over an organization in a turnaround mode, I immediately moved to a 7:30 a.m. standing meeting to review the metrics of the organization. In many cases we would start with the inventory method I described and work our way

Meet more fre-
quently to change
behavior more
quickly.

from there. The meeting simply focused on our day-to-day performance as a team and the individual units as well. It never
ceased to amaze me how little people knew about their own
departments and how little teamwork there truly was amongst the
staff. I had all the support groups there as well as the line managers. Two things would happen: The team would begin to gel,
and the weaker players self-identified every time.

I recall taking over a real disaster of an area with major backlogs
and procedural breaks, failed audits, and expense overruns. What
amazed me about the first day's meeting was how clueless the
team was about its own performance. There was zero accountability, and all they were focused on was the past—how bad it was
and how terrible the previous management team was. After a few
days we began talking about the current tasks at hand, then came
our performance as the days went by, and we began to see
accountability right before our eyes. People would make com-
mitments and either keep them or break them, but we would
review them every day. Suddenly, the organization picked up the
pace—I mean literally as well. People moved faster because they
all knew that the next morning at 7:30 a.m., it was review time.
People's knowledge and understanding began to grow of the
things they did. They brought forward the issues and obstacles,
and the focus was on success.

The meetings did not go very deeply into any one area or topic,
but they would set the stage for such meetings to discuss the
appropriate topics at greater length. They would help us prioritize the workloads and keep the communication flowing in real
time. There were fewer emails and voicemails and fewer instances
of "I'll get back to you" because people were there the next
morning and were accountable.

On a monthly basis we would get together in a conference room
for four to six hours and pour over the business, with broad discussions on tactical approaches, strategic discussions, and a more
in-depth review of the business. There were also specific topics
or issues we referred to as "deep dives," where we took a single
topic and reviewed and discussed it. Sometimes it was a problem,
and we would brainstorm the solutions; other times it was a strategy on how to handle a potential or current issue. The depth of
those meetings was needed because the design of those discussions was to produce a direction or an action. Managers knew
they could request, call, or recommend such a session—it was,
after all, part of our management process.

Using Committees

Any management process needs governance and a monitoring vehicle. In larger organizations we formed committees; in smaller organizations we did cross-functional reviews. In any case, it was a group of people coming together with a specific charter and set of activities to ensure that policies were being followed and observed or that decisions were being made. Sometimes it was both!

Where committees go wrong is when they don't have a charter or an operating protocol, so they end up being an endless discussion where people voice concerns and opinions but nothing gets accomplished. The first step in forming a committee is deciding how the committee structure will fit into your process—or perhaps it doesn't apply. If you want or need to obtain an independent view of a particular discipline—audit, projects, product development—or you need to create focus and accountability on an area balance sheet, reserves, or fixed assets, you can establish a committee to do so, provided that the committee has a specific charter and a process that it will go through and that it reports to you and you senior team the results each time it meets.

A committee must plug into the overall management process at the right time and sequence for it to be value-added. Picture a pyramid (see Figure 5.5). At the top of the pyramid is your

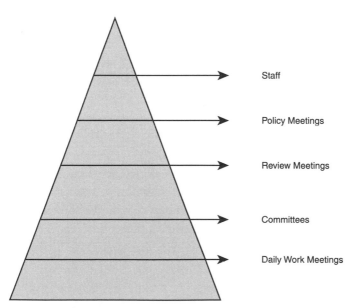

Figure 5.5
Corporate meeting pyramid.

Staff

Policy Meetings

Review Meetings

Committees

Daily Work Meetings

Make sure committees plug into the management process at the right time and sequence.

management team. Its focus is on the vital few issues that run a department or organization as well as the strategy needed to obtain the vision. Below that are various committees whose role it is to monitor and govern the discipline you have assigned to them—not to run it, but to govern it. A committee like your staff meeting gathers information, but they gather it on a specific topic. They are a "depth" focus, and out of their review and discussion comes a seal of approval, a policy change, or creation and accountability.

I require my committee chairpersons not only to keep minutes but also to provide us with a chairpersons' memo that discusses the committee focus and tells the organization how well the function they are governing is performing, where it needs to be fixed, and what recommendations they have to fix it. Some committees produce a report (not minutes) on the topics they are responsible for that is discussed at my staff meetings.

You might say, "That is great, but I am a unit manager of 10 people." Let me share something with you. When I was an assistant supervisor at 24 years old, I had one direct report. *One!* He and I wanted to improve the report that we did for the company we were at. Our job was to audit the inventory accounting department and write a report (literally a book) on the variations in inventory levels that were unaccounted for. We decided that we would meet every Wednesday afternoon to brainstorm how we could improve the report. Some weeks we'd invite the technology guy we knew; other weeks it was an accountant or a phone meeting with an inventory manager in the field. We took notes, and then we would take a Wednesday and sit down to review our notes and see what we could implement. That was my first-ever "committee"—outside of the line of fire, laser-focused on one thing and going deep to understand it, finally reporting out (the notes), and deciding what to improve in the report as well as how and when.

A committee is simply a group of people with a common goal who have the expertise and assignment to focus on a single thread and ensure it is working the best way it can to fulfill the strategic vision of the organization.

I think you now have a framework to understand and implement a management process. However big or small your area may be, one sure thing is that you need a management process.

Chapter 6

Performance Management

- The Importance of Communication
- The Importance of Positive Feedback
- Giving Feedback
- Setting Expectations
- Communicating Time
- Considering Capability and Attainable Goals
- The Performance Discussion

When I was coming up through the corporate ranks, I recall a speech that the chairman was making to a group of the top 200 people in the company I worked for. Over and over in that speech he said, "As a manager you manage two things— human resources and capital resources." Never have truer words been uttered in the corporate arena. There are many books on performance management, and many consultants and programs have made their way into performance management over the years. All of them focus on different aspects with catch phrases and acronyms, and when you peel away the gadgets, forms, books, and studies, performance management comes down to a few basics.

- Set clear and realistic expectations.
- Verify that the expectations are understood.
- Agree on and quantify what success looks like.
- Monitor progress.
- Give feedback (both positive and negative) along the way every chance you can.

The Importance of Communication

The issue in performance management is always communication. I remember sitting down with my new manager when I took over an area, and she said to me, "I want this to be the best finance area it can be. I know it has shortcomings, but I think with the right leadership it could perform better." She said it, and I heard it.

Be clear about your expectations regarding performance.

We later had a mid-year review, which was the company's practice. I felt pretty good going into it, mainly because my unit, although not making all its goals, was quite frankly the best it could be! But in that review, my manager told me that I was not meeting her expectations and gave me an example: "By now I thought you would have fired Mike, replaced him, and moved Sandy to a different job." I responded that I had heard her tell me to make the current unit the best it could be, and while I agreed with her point on the people, I didn't think I had an option to move folks out.

We had never really agreed on what "the best it could be" meant. The expectation wasn't clear, and that is how you often get to a point where your view of performance differs from that of the person you are managing. You need to be clear about what you expect and how you expect it will be done.

I had a manager who hit every deliverable I gave him, ran under his expense targets, and was well regarded by his peers. One issue he had, however, was that his people hated him, and his turnover rate validated that. So what do you think his performance grade was? If you think about a manager and the "two resources" approach, he was a 50-percent performer.

Get in the habit of talking to your team daily about performance, both good and bad. As the manager, you are setting the standard of feedback, and people want to know how they are doing. Many organizations do annual reviews, and I can tell you that as a manager, they do not serve you well. A quarterly sit-down is the minimal feedback model in today's world.

Talk to your team about performance daily.

The Importance of Positive Feedback

Often people associate performance management with negative feedback, when in actuality feedback has greater value when it is positive. People want to know what they do right so they can keep doing it and export the thought process to other areas of their responsibility. One of the greatest lessons I learned in performance management occurred when I was named the head of technology at a particular company.

Focus on positive feedback instead of negative.

My very first day on the job, our payroll system went down, and—you guessed it—it was payday! We could not determine the cause and therefore the solution, so I gathered the application team into a conference room and began analyzing what went wrong with the system. As we were discussing the problem, my administrative assistant came into the room and said my boss was on the line and wanted to speak to me as soon as possible. When I got on the phone, he asked me what was happening. I explained that the system went down, I had all the people responsible for the system in a room, and we were working on the issue. He paused and then said, "What makes you think that the people who created the problem could solve it? If they could, they wouldn't have created it in the first place!"

He suggested that I bring into the room my top-rated people in the technology department as defined by our review processes. I did just that, and the results were amazing to watch. I had about six additional people, all top-rated performers by their managers, join us. They began to ask questions and understand the issue, and in a matter of a few hours, we had the root cause and the solution. The top performers brought a perspective that the others simply did not have. They also spoke from their own frame of reference and assimilated their experiences into the problem at hand.

It turns out that the system deployment was into a test region that lacked certain connections to downstream systems. One of the top performers stumbled on that when he asked, "What steps did you go through to move into production?" and the response was, "We didn't have to move it into a new system environment because this region was live to begin with." He quickly corrected the speaker and said that infrastructure regions were never live and that the plan to move that region to live had been delayed a few weeks. We moved the system into a live region, and the paychecks began flowing!

Top performance is contagious. You just need to call it out as a manager so others can catch it!

Giving Feedback

Discuss both positives and negatives in the interest of self-improvement.

Managing performance is essentially coaching and should be viewed as such. Great coaches call timeouts and discuss performance all the time—in fact, sports limit timeouts because they are a weapon to gain an advantage. So, too, is this true in business. Going over a project in terms of what went well and what didn't should be a part of every project. Discuss both the successful ones and the unsuccessful ones. That is a best practice for self-improvement.

Here is how I like to manage and coach performance.

1. List out the critical things you value in performance—maybe there are 10 of them.

2. Discuss each one with your employee, noting what success looks like for each one—the clearer the better.

3. Across the top of the list, create a scale from 1 to 5, with 5 being the best and 1 being the worst.

4. Give your employee a copy of that list, and you keep one, too.

At any time during the course of your performance management cycle, each of you should be able to call for a touch-base meeting. When you do, both of you should independently fill out the form, come to the meeting, and have a discussion that calibrates the performance. Focus on the gaps separately; those gaps where you think the employee is a 1 and he thinks he is a 4 need the most discussion. But every rating needs some discussion.

I once used this approach with an employee, and she rated herself a 5 in communications, whereas I had her as a 3. When we began discussing that, the problem became obvious to both of us. She viewed communications as her communicating with her employees and with me. I, on the other hand, added an additional group—her peers. It wasn't that she was not a good communicator—actually, she was a very good communicator—it was that her view of communications was too narrow as the leader of the area, in my view. She made the adjustment, and we went on from there.

I could never imagine that going on for a year while I waited for the review process. It would be like getting one report card at the end of the year in grade school to tell you whether you passed.

Every project manager in my organization gets a review session after the project is concluded and at some point while it is in process. We never go more than 90 days without performance feedback.

When I ask managers why they do not give feedback, they often tell me it is because they are uncomfortable with the discussion. That is like a coach saying, "I do not like to call a timeout in a game because I am uncomfortable." Giving feedback is part of being a manager. If an individual doesn't performance coach, then he or she shouldn't be a manager.

> As a manager, you will need to become comfortable providing feedback.

Setting Expectations

Setting clear expectations is pivotal to creating top performance. Expectation-setting involves a few things. First, it requires a statement of what is expected, followed by a discussion to place the expectation in context. "I want you to achieve a unit cost of $500 per unit" is an expectation. It is clear, and it is measurable. Let's assume the employee has the tools to achieve it. If you think you have enough here, you are wrong. The discussion needs to take place regarding what $500 per unit looks like.

> Be sure to state what is expected and place it in context.

I once gave a financial target to a manager similar to the $500 per unit example. I was clear on it, and she understood it so she left my office to go conquer the world! She was in an organization that dealt with customer service refunds. We had a threshold that for cases of less than $50, we would refund the customer because, frankly, it wasn't worth the cost to research it. Her idea was to raise that threshold to $150, reduce the research staff, and meet the unit cost goal. What she missed was the fact that our refund rate on items more than $100 was less than 10 percent. In fact, on items more than $100, we only refunded about 2 percent and kept 98 percent as income for the company, so the math changed on the tradeoff after $100.

So here's the quick math. Our unit cost prior to the goal of $500 per unit was $515 per unit. So we needed to reduce our cost by $15 per unit to meet the goal. Each month we processed about 10,000 units. That means we spent $5,150,000 to process in a month.

We also handled about 1,500 refund items in total, of which 1,200 were above the $100 threshold that changed the ratio, but all the 1,200 were below the manager's new threshold and would be written off without any research. (Hence we let go of the research department.) The average cost on the 1,200 was $145.

Ready for some math? We wrote off 1,200 items at $145, or $174,000. We "saved" $150,000 in labor cost. So she hit the expense goal, we saved $150,000, and we gave up $174,000 in the process! One adjustment here for the accountants reading this: We really only would save 98 percent of that $174,000 because we would end up writing it off 2 percent even after we researched it. And 98 percent of $174,000 is $170,520!

Now, before you tell me how dumb she was, let me remind you of something. Her goal was to hit $500 per unit. I can just hear you say, "Yeah but..."—but nothing! Our expectation was not clear.

If we discussed that expectation and what success looked like, I might have said, "We need to hit all our standards for quality and revenues, as well as reduce our cost."

Suppose you have an employee who meets every goal you have asked him to, and in a manner where he does not cut corners or make poor tradeoffs, but he does not manage people well and creates turnover as a result. Did he meet the goals? Not if one of them was to manage people and conduct himself within the values you have defined. Setting expectations always requires discussion and envisioning success.

Communicating Time

The other key to performance management is time. I remember asking my son one evening to take out the garbage. In my neighborhood the garbage man comes at about 7:00 a.m., so the idea is to have the garbage on the curb waiting for him before then! My son was watching a football game at the time, lying on the floor as young teenagers tend to do, and he responded with a soft grunt of "Okay." About 10 minutes went by, I asked again, and he of course replied again with a resounding "Okay."

An additional 10 minutes went by, and I took a more authoritative tone this time and said, "Are you going to take out the garbage or not?" To which he replied in genuine and total amazement, "You mean right now?" I countered with, "Of course I mean right now! When did you think I meant?" To which he stated a true fact: "I don't know. You didn't say, so I figured I had until 7 in the morning." And you know what? He was right. (By the way, I just invoked the classic "parents are always correct" rule, raised my voice slightly, and said, "Take it out." He did, but if he is reading this, he now—and only now—knows that he was right and I was wrong!)

I was judging performance on a factor and expectation that I had not communicated. We were not aligned on what success looked like for that goal. How many times do you see this situation in management, where an expectation exists that is not explicit, not understood, or not aligned appropriately? That is what clarity is all about. Generally, time and definition are the two killers in performance management that need clarity.

> Good performance management requires clarity about time as well as definition.

Considering Capability and Attainable Goals

A remaining issue is usually capability. Can the person achieve what you are asking? If the person cannot, what tools does he need in order to accomplish the goal? You simply need to ask the question, "Do you have what you need to get the job done?" As a manager, you owe it to your employee to set expectations that are attainable. They may be difficult, taxing, stretching, and even on the edge, but they must always be attainable.

> Performance expectations should always be attainable for the employee.

If you discipline yourself to attainable goals, then feedback becomes an easy part of the process. Once you have a performance plan, you need to schedule regular feedback sessions, and it is often best to schedule formal feedback sessions well in advance so both you and the employee know that you have set aside time specifically for feedback. In between those sessions, it is always good to point out any positives you want to reinforce and negatives you want to work on as you go.

I was once given performance feedback that I needed to listen more carefully at meetings and focus more on the issues at hand. My boss at the time told me to put a pen on the table and to point the pen away from me when I spoke and at me when I listened. A few weeks later I was in a meeting with him, and after the meeting he congratulated me on how intently I listened to the people in the meeting. He also noticed I was using his pen trick to help me balance talking and listening. Of course that made me feel good, because I was accomplishing what I set out to do. That type of reinforcement builds people's success.

Immediate feedback and reinforcement can be very powerful tools.

I also recall that after a meeting where I didn't do so well, he simply said to me, "That meeting was an example of what I want you to change. You hardly listened to folks' ideas before jumping in, and you were introducing tangents that were off focus." Having just gone through the meeting, I could see exactly what he was talking about. That type of immediate feedback is very powerful.

The Performance Discussion

Finally, there is the actual performance discussion itself. You need to prepare yourself for the discussion. You should jot down the positive points of the performance and the areas of opportunity you see. Put a range of time next to each and leave a place to write down the reaction to your observations. Rather than interrupt, write down your reaction and comments, but always let the employee finish speaking so you understand the key points he or she is making. To the degree that you can, you should use specific examples and references to behaviors. Choose your words carefully. That is why preparation is so important—it's best to ask questions about why than to draw your own conclusions.

I once had a situation in which a very heavyset woman would always go to the copier the long way around the office instead of taking a more direct route. The assistant supervisor of that group said to me, "She always takes the longest path to get to the copier. Same thing when she goes and comes for lunch; she just wastes time any way she can." I decided to call the woman into my office and ask her why she chose the seemingly longest path every time she left her desk. She replied that the doctor had advised her to take the longest routes from point to point to maximize her circulation. She had diabetes and was overweight, and she needed to move to improve her circulation and health. The lesson here is to not jump to conclusions about behaviors—ask.

Suppose you have an employee who isn't contributing in meetings. One way to ask about this would be, "I noticed you are very quiet in our meetings. Is there a reason for that?" That is more effective than, "You need to speak up in our meetings." The first way you create the coaching opportunity; the second way you state the obvious, but there is little chance that you get to the source. Create the coaching moment.

> Ask questions when in doubt—do not automatically make assumptions.

Every review or feedback session needs an action plan where, as an employee's coach, you commit to helping. In turn, the employee commits to a behavior modification. You then have a common basis for improving and coaching.

Finally, with the plan developed and documented, you can begin to create opportunities for improvement as you manage your unit. I had an individual who was poor at public speaking; he was nervous and had a poor presentation style in general. I identified this as an area he needed to improve, and he agreed but shared with me that he was intimidated in front of groups.

I began to coach him on public speaking as part of our weekly one-on-one. We selected a report that he would give at a staff meeting, and for three weeks he came to my office every week and went through the report. I would role-play it with him, and we would talk about the points he needed to make and also about how to ease himself into speaking.

In staff meetings or other meetings we were in, I would always be sure to ask him an open-ended question to give him a chance to speak publicly. I would then debrief with him, and over time he became more comfortable. He never really loved public speaking, but it no longer was a weak point in his skill set.

> **KEYS TO A GREAT PERFORMANCE REVIEW**
> 1. List the points you will discuss.
> 2. Determine an approximate time for each.
> 3. Stick to the facts.
> 4. Ask why.
> 5. Create an action plan.

Not all performance coaching has a happy ending; you owe it to the individual, yourself, and your team to identify performance issues and move quickly to correct them or to move the person out of the job. Remember, everyone sees what you see. The longer you tolerate poor performance, the harder it is to manage good performers.

I can think of many cases where I stayed with a performer for too long, especially when I began to coach them and became biased toward a positive outcome. Set a time parameter for the performance to change and then honor it for yourself and for the individual. If it does not work out, then treat the person with respect and dignity and be professional, but conclude the employment for everyone's sake.

Chapter 7

Environment

- Positive Environments
- Creating an Environment for Success
- Adapting the Environment to Reflect Your Vision, Mission, and Values
- Using Rewards and Recognition
- Tailoring an Environment
- Don't Forget the External Environment!

As a manager, one of the most critical things you manage is the environment in which your employees work. The environment people work in creates the atmosphere, tone, and pace that we call the *workplace*. When people like the environment they work in, they extend that to the customers and co-workers they interact with, and that produces results. Have you ever seen an environment where people enjoy what they do?

Positive Environments

I was driving to work one day, and I was getting ready to stop in for my morning cup of coffee, as I always did, at a particular convenience store when I noticed a new doughnut store, Krispy Kreme. I decided to go in and try it out.

When I walked in, I noticed that the store had a wide-open layout and looked like a factory of some kind. There were doughnut makers shouting "Doughnuts up!" and "Tray ready!" and other doughnut terms. All the employees had hats and were dressed the same, and they were smiling and talking. As I got in line, a young girl came up to me carrying a tray with cups and a pot of coffee. "Can I offer you a cup of coffee, sir?" she greeted me with a smile. I responded, "Sure." Now I was holding a cup of coffee, and another girl came over to me with doughnuts and asked if I'd care for a doughnut as well.

By time I came to the register to order, I had my coffee and a delicious hot doughnut. The girl behind the counter looked me in the eye, tilted her head to one side, smiled from ear to ear, and said, "How many dozen would you like, sir?" I paused for about five or six seconds and said, "Two." I left the store with 24 glazed doughnuts. I was a hero of sorts at work, but it was because the environment in that store was more than a doughnut shop—it was an experience!

Disney is a classic example of an environment, whether you are at one of their parks or in one of their retail stores. Apple provides another example—they create an environment for buying a computer or accessories at one of their stores. These are companies that sell the *experience* of buying along with the products. It's the same in the workplace.

If your employee satisfaction rating is high, I guarantee you that your customer satisfaction and your productivity will be high as well.

Creating an Environment for Success

The environment you create, reinforce, and manage every day, along with your selection of the right people, tools, and performance management, will determine your success. Of these key management focuses, the toughest one to understand, master, and manage is the environment. After all, this is not taught in any business school (although it should be), nor is it openly discussed in management forums or boardrooms across America. So, let's discuss it in depth here.

The environment you create is tied to your vision, mission, and values. It must reinforce those and bring energy into the workplace that surrounds what you believe, the activities you pursue, and the manner in which you pursue them.

The environment is made up of the physical workplace, the guidelines that exist for behavior, and the conduct created, modeled, and accepted. I ran a call center in the '90s, and one of the first things I did was to take down all of the artwork in that call center and replace it with our company's advertising and marketing messages. In addition, we placed our mission statement, vision, and values throughout the center. We painted the walls the colors of the company as well. This created an environment of pride and fun throughout the center. We also posted the top performers and their statistics in a special area called the "Wall of Fame," and on casual days we gave out company logo apparel to top performers that could be worn any day as "wildcards."

We had organized the center into pods that were previously numbered 1 to 20. We had a pod-naming contest, and each group personally named their pod. We supplied banners over each pod to proudly show off their new names. We did things like have contests to keep people highly engaged. For example, in March we ran our own version of March maleness [sic], the NCAA Basketball Tournament. We took the team statistics each week and used them as points that determined the winners of the pairings and the progress of the teams.

You could almost feel the electricity of the call center when you walked in. We would take people on tours of our call center, and they were consistently amazed at how much fun our people were having working there. They often would say, "How can I get a job here?" Many times, they referred family members to us for employment.

Our productivity was among the best in the company, our employee satisfaction was the highest, and our customer satisfaction was among the best.

Of course, this was one element of the equation; we still had to hire the right people, figure out the process maps, give people the tools, train them, and manage their performance. The environment, however, is an element that can separate you from the pack and create momentum around your organization. There is no single environment that is better or more productive than another; there is only one thing to consider, and that is what type of environment reflects your vision, mission, and values.

In the early '90s, I ran an operations processing center with a much different environment. There we were focused on professional delivery of our service and valued knowledge of our products and expertise in our industry. In that operations center, we had cubicles with higher walls and glass partitions. There we did have artwork—it was black and white and had a historic tone to it. We did not have a paging system; rather, we had a desk phone notification system. The operating center was quiet, and as a result our staff was very formal and deliberate. When we would tour senior management through that operating center, they would always comment, "Are you sure this is an operating center?"

Adapting the Environment to Reflect Your Vision, Mission, and Values

Regardless of the vision, mission, or values you are trying to support, every aspect of the environment needs to reflect them.

The Physical Environment

To begin with there is the actual physical environment, and depending on what you can control, you can change every aspect of your environment or just a few. Regardless, change what you can afford to change. One example is what you have on the walls around you. To create pride and company spirit, you may want to use marketing advertisements and posters. If you don't control the walls, you certainly can control the bulletin board, so think about what you want that board to convey. In a sales environment it may be a contest ranking, top performers, or product sales. In an operating environment it may be productivity statistics and customer appreciation letters—the types of behaviors that reflect the mission and vision of what you are trying to achieve and the results that show the progress.

You may also display your vision, mission, and values on posters or banners or even on notepads or various trinkets, such as paperweights or other desk items (mouse pads, portfolios, and so on). People take pride in having possessions with the company name or department name, from T-shirts to jackets—it's all about reinforcing the message and creating ownership and identity for the mission.

The Dynamic of the Environment

That is the physical part of the environment, but how do you create the dynamic of the environment—the interaction of people in a manner that is conducive to productivity, pride, and accomplishment that will enable you to meet your goals? Once again, it depends on your goals, but the golden rule is this: What you think about you talk about, and what you talk about you bring about.

Rule to live by: What you think about you talk about, and what you talk about you bring about.

As the leader or manager of the area, you must talk about what you are trying to accomplish every day to everyone you can. You need to sell or get people to buy into what you are trying to bring about, you need to engage people in what you want to get done, and you need to call out behaviors and accomplishments that others can see and emulate in the workplace.

Every day at about 3:00 p.m., I take a walk through the organization. It takes about 20 minutes; I stop at a desk or two, I read the bulletin board, I greet folks and ask how they are, maybe get a story about the picture on their desk or recognize them in a small way with a thank you, answer a general question or two, and reinforce their supervisor or manager with a smile or a wave that lets people know that I know the manager and support him or her.

I encourage my managers to know their people and have frequent staff meetings, floor meetings, contests, and so on. These interactions should all be connected and related to achieving the mission—no activity is without a connection to the mission.

Every activity should be connected to the mission.

The result is an endless stream of reinforcement, greater understanding, and participation in achieving the goal.

What makes up the environment? Managers often overlook the makeup of the workplace and miss the opportunity to establish an atmosphere that is not only conducive to high performance, but that reinforces the vision, mission, and values while inviting people to engage and get results. Posting goals and tracking them publicly is great, but combining that with a meeting to go over the posting reinforces the goals and makes the posting come alive. Posting top performers or customer letters has the same impact—it brings to life behaviors and goals that are often talked about but that people don't always get to see in play.

Using Rewards and Recognition

All recognition and reward strategies must reinforce the vision, mission, and values of the unit or company.

Rewards and recognition are a critical part of any workplace environment. What behaviors will you recognize and what behaviors will you reward? To begin with, any recognition and reward strategy needs to reinforce the vision, mission, and values; otherwise, you will not accomplish your goal as the manager. Remember, you want all activity and interaction in your department aimed at achieving your goals.

There are many types of reward and recognition that can help you achieve goals, but to begin with, you should understand the difference between the two.

Recognition

Recognition is drawing people's attention to a behavior you want to be repeated.

Recognition is about awareness—making people aware of a behavior you would like to see repeated. You reinforce it by calling it to everyone's attention and communicating that it was a good thing. Let's face it; people want to do well. No one I know comes to work to get fired or to fail. Conversely, they all want to get promoted, so recognition is a way of telling them how.

The beauty of recognition is that it is easy, it costs very little, and everyone can do it. In today's electronic age, you can easily promote recognition in your area. For example, you can produce a recognition email, much like an electronic greeting card, and place it on your technology server for people to access. Define what behaviors you want them to recognize, and ask them to send the email when they see the behavior. You can expand this to have a copy automatically mailed to the supervisor or manager of the area, track how many people get it, publish the names of those who get the most recognition, and even give small awards or certificates to the recipients.

Now imagine that process, but let's include some internal marketing. Suppose your company values are: a) Always do the right thing; b) Add value in everything you do; c) Be professional; and d) Make things easier for the customers.

Now you can have four forms of recognition emails: The Right Thing!, Value Added!, You're a Pro!, and Customer Service!

You can unleash the recognition of values in the workplace and participate in it yourself. You can create rewards, contests, and public recognition posts on boards, electronic messaging, and even your internal website. At town hall meetings, staff meetings, or even special recognition lunch meetings, you can recognize your employees who exhibit the behaviors.

And yes, you will always have someone who beats the system, plays around it, and attempts to break it. Here is some sound advice: When it comes to behaviors, play to the majority and be relentless in your commitment to the behavior, and eventually the majority will squeeze out the few or the minority.

You must be relentless in your commitment to the desired behavior.

Recognition at this level and intensity is not a new concept; it just is a forgotten one, from what I see in the workplace. It is often viewed as the soft stuff by senior executives who do not want such programs distracting the employees or who view these as not paying back. These are the same executives who do not understand why their customer service is so low, why employee morale is low, and why their people simply do not understand what they want them to do. These executives often are good at starting the fire by providing the spark—maybe they bring in a motivational speaker to "charge up" their teams, only to see the energy drain as soon as the speaking engagement ends. What they are missing is the reinforcement that reward and recognition plays. Reward and recognition provide the continual stroke of the flame that allows it to catch on and spread throughout the organization.

Such executives are missing the point of creating an environment. Did you ever see a professional sports team right before a big game? There is usually a motivational moment that ends in a crescendo of chanting, screaming, and jumping and then they take the field. If you listen carefully, the chanting and screaming is not random—it is always the same, and it is themed to the behavior. In football, you hear the defense yelling and chanting things like, "Bend but don't break" or "We can't be beat" or "The train stops here!" These are mental reinforcements about their beliefs and values about playing defense.

Can you imagine screaming and chanting each morning before you began to work? Gathering your department around you and screaming things such as, "Who helps the customer? We do!" Or "We add value to the bottom line!" Or "Productivity, productivity, productivity!" Probably not, but you would love to have the same level of intensity and energy, wouldn't you? That is what managing an environment can do for you.

During the Christmas holiday a few years ago, we had a Toys for Tots program where folks would bring in toys, and we would invite the Marines to the office and present them with the bundle of toys. At the same time we ran a contest where the top-producing department for the month would get $1,000 gift certificate to Toys 'R Us to be used for the Toys for Tots program. The winners would go to Toys 'R Us and go on a shopping spree, and they would actually do the presentation to the Marines.

This way a great way to reinforce the values we had as an organization and tie it to the mission and what we were about in a way that helped the community. That is what an environment is all about—creating energy and activity that brings to life what you are trying to accomplish.

Reward

Reward is typically related to pay—it is a promotion, an increase, a raise, or a bonus. Unlike recognition, reward is a contract of sorts between an employer and his or her employees that lays out goals, objectives, and the reward the employee will receive should he or she attain those goals.

Typically at the beginning of a cycle—perhaps the beginning of the year or quarter—management lays out the expectations that it has for employee performance and also lays out the reward for achieving those objectives.

You have to be careful with rewards, because you will always get exactly what you pay for, and you may not always want it.

Rewards are typically (but not always) related to pay.

I ran an operating center in the '80s, and we closed mortgage loans for customers. When I took on the area of responsibility, the incentive pay or reward for employees was based on the number of loans each person closed. And boy, did that group close loans! The problem was that they closed them regardless of whether they should close them! There were certain rules that ensured the quality of the mortgage and the perfection of the mortgage as a financial instrument that could then be sold to an investor later on in the process, and these were rarely followed because they interfered with the closing of the loan. The reward was not aligned with the desired result—a golden rule of rewards. The first thing we did as a team was to align the quality of what we did with the quantity of what we did. We calculated pay on closed loans as we always had but made one slight adjustment: We multiplied the number of closed loans by the percentage score that closed correctly.

So if you closed 100 loans but got 75 percent of them correctly done, you were paid on 75 percent of 100 loans, or 75 loans. Suddenly, the quality of what we did improved dramatically. Reward aligned with goals equals desired result!

One of the keys to rewarding behavior is to ensure that the process you are asking people to undertake will indeed create the desired result—a concept that I call *procedural justice*. In other words, if employees follow the rules, they win and the company wins. Sounds pretty simple, doesn't it?

> Reward must be aligned with goals to achieve a desired result.

In the fourth quarter of 1999, my operating center had a goal of 95-percent customer satisfaction, meaning that on the surveys we sent out to customers, if 95 out of 100 said they were satisfied with our service, we would pay each employee a bonus of $800. Pretty good for an operating center where the average employee made about $25,000 per year in base salary—this would of course be over and above base salary.

That year we decided to roll out our new system in the fourth quarter, and it was an ugly rollout. The system was down more than it was up in the first 30 days—data corruption issues, system performance issues—in short, it was a mess. Finally, after about 60 days, we had worked out all the kinks, and life was good again.

That quarter when the customer survey came out, we scored 76 percent, the lowest we ever scored as an operating center. It was obvious that the system issues had hindered our performance and cratered our score. So here's the question: Do you pay out to people? After all, they did not achieve the objective, and it is a slippery slope in rewards when you do not adhere to the goals and you begin to pay out on subjectivity. In fact, you should never pay out on subjectivity if the goal itself was not a subjective one, but rather a clearly defined, measurable, and attainable goal.

> When implementing rewards, you must adhere to the goals and avoid paying out on subjectivity.

But in this case the employees could not achieve the goal because we, the management, inadvertently took away their tools when we introduced a system that didn't work.

The solution we came up with was to, as they say in Las Vegas, let it ride, so the next quarter payout was doubled if the goal was achieved.

The end result was not surprising to any student of reward—our satisfaction was 97 percent, the highest we ever achieved! Even long afterward, 97 percent was still the best, and I believe it probably still is!

Setting goals and expectations that are associated with the rewards is critical—they must be aligned with your vision and mission, and they absolutely need to produce the desired result. I always leave about 25 percent of a bonus or reward for a subjective measure—the *how* versus the *what* you accomplish. This helps keep the values and the environmental issues in the forefront, as well as the harder business goals and metrics, and it leaves you some room to adjust to market or external factors.

Communication is also critical to your rewards strategy. If you don't communicate your goals and the associated rewards to your team, they won't be able to achieve the vision and goal!

I once had the assignment of converting an entire sales force from manual submissions of sales orders to electronic submissions. Each member of the sales team was given a laptop, training courses, manager-led reinforcement meetings, help desk support and daily reminders, best practices, and frequently asked questions feedback. Yet, the fraction of the sales force that used the laptops was only about 63 percent.

It wasn't that the system didn't work or wasn't efficient. And when I would go out to the field, people would tell me, "It's taking time," or that they just didn't like this new way, but would give it a try.

When I told my boss that we were fully deployed but our usage rate was 63 percent, he had a few questions. Once he was convinced that the system worked well and was achieving the results we had envisioned for productivity, cost, and service, he asked me, "Is it clear to the sales force that we want them only on electronic submissions?"

I thought for a moment and said, "Yes. I spoke about the communications plan we had, market visits, some fun awards we had for the early adopters, contests, and showcase efforts...."

Then he asked me, "Do we pay commission on manual submissions?" I nodded and said yes, but I got it right then. Communications is not only what you say; it is what you do and how you reinforce it in your behavior in the daily running of your business that creates clarity.

I announced to the team that in 60 days we would no longer pay commission on any manual submissions. There was a bit of an uproar, followed by a list of what we needed in training and equipment changes to make the system more efficient. Suddenly, it was clear that we were going to electronic submissions! Within 60 days our usage was 98 percent, and within 90 days it was 100 percent. Clarity of communications in what you say and what you do to reinforce it is critical.

Giving people a place to ask questions unencumbered by concerns will allow you to do two things—bring clarity to the work environment and also get insight into the work environment.

The sharing of the response is critical, because many folks have the same questions. In addition, it gives you the platform to expand the answers to reinforce the message of the communication and the overall culture.

Most importantly, it increases the velocity by which a team or an organization runs. Simply put, it increases speed to the goal because it aligns people in the same direction with a clear understanding of how to get there.

Managers often worry about giving the answers people want to hear. I will make two points about that. First, if it is the answer people want to hear, why isn't it the right one? Second and perhaps related, if it is not the right answer, what do you know that they don't?

I was once asked by a salesperson in an open forum why we didn't pay more for a certain type of product sale. The product was more complex to sell, took longer, and was more profitable. I did not really know the answer, so I told them that I didn't know but I would take it up with my management team.

After the forum was over, I met with my team to debrief them on the forum. When we got to this topic, the head of compensation replied on behalf of the group that they had no way of tracking on a "by product" basis, and until now they had really never opened it up to discussion. I waited, and my CFO spoke next and said, "Well, why would we want to pay more and reduce the margin on our best product? That is financial suicide."

Finally my head of sales spoke. "It's no big deal. This always comes up, and no one quits over it. No competitors do it, so we really shouldn't—our margins are thin overall."

So I said, "If we were to pay commissions by product based on the activity and complexity—which, by the way, is what the sales force indirectly is suggesting—what would that look like?"

At our next sales forum, we explored the idea of matching the margins of the products to the commission structure. Surprisingly, the room was divided about 60/40 in favor of moving to such a structure. We explored a bit further using focus groups, and exactly two years after that question was asked, we had a new compensation plan supported by a new system that set us apart in the industry and had us focused on revenue generation versus volume in the sales force. Oddly enough, we increased our volumes and profits the first year we implemented the compensation plan.

It all stemmed from a single question and a thoughtful dialogue around the answer and rewarding the desired behavior.

Tailoring an Environment

What do you want people to say about working for you?

To begin to approach the environment question, you need to ask yourself what you want people to say about working for you. If you are really committed, you should ask your employees what makes a great working environment and then begin to tailor your environment to how people like to work.

I ran a document-processing department—an area that basically checked documents against screen images to verify that the key information was successfully transferred and that the formats were correct. In addition, the employees then filed the documents in a bin.

I would say the average age of the employees in that department was about 22 years old, with many part-time college or two-year-degree beginners in the area. I was talking to the supervisor one day, and she told me that many of the employees were asking whether they could listen to CDs while they filed. It was the '90s, and Discmans (the precursor to iPods) were fairly popular. I asked her what she thought about that, and her response was that she thought it was unprofessional. These were people who worked in the basement and never saw customers or talked on the phone—in fact, we didn't have any phones in the department, though there were a few in the conference rooms.

I simply said, "Exactly what do you mean by 'professional'? Have we created a professional environment here for these people to work in?" She hesitated a bit and then said what she meant was respectful. "Okay," I said, "I agree with that, but how would listening to a CD with earphones on be disrespectful?" She thought a minute and said, "Well, they would probably start dancing around or something." I just looked at her, and we both started laughing.

We decided to bring the department together and discussed our concerns about bringing the CD era into the department. We were concerned that the productivity would drop, the quality would drop, and people would not respect the environment, but we agreed to do a test and track such things with a sample group of randomly selected employees.

In a short period of time, we had our answer. Productivity went up by 12 percent, quality scores improved, and employee satisfaction was obviously up. More importantly, people enjoyed what they were doing—they liked coming to work.

The reason that it worked was twofold. First, we gave people what they wanted in their everyday environment—note it was what *they* wanted, not what *management* wanted in the everyday workplace. It didn't conflict with anything we were trying to accomplish, so we were willing to give it a try. We also defined success to the team, and they understood it and delivered. They owned the results, and that made a huge difference.

You would be amazed at what the physical environment can do for the morale and the productivity of a department. Company posters reinforcing values, goals, or objectives versus the usual sterile corporate artwork literally liven up the unit and get energy moving. Daily statistics, winners of work awards, and pictures of people in the workplace create a friendly environment and help people feel more comfortable, and when people are in their comfort zone, they are more productive.

Comfortable employees are productive employees.

The environment should reflect your vision, mission, and values as well as your business. High-volume service-oriented businesses need a lively environment where employees are able to have a good time and create energy. Employees will convey the same energy to their customers and work as a team much more freely because they will interact more in that type of environment.

I worked in a collections center at one point in my career, and when I first took over the area, it had a very low collective morale. People hardly spoke to each other. The physical workplace was terrible—beige walls, no pictures, and empty bulletin boards with only fair labor laws posted were the extent of the décor.

When I inquired about why this was such a dismal-looking place, the supervisor replied, "We are a collections center; this is no place for fun." The employees actually hated the place; there was no pride, no interaction between people, and in general it was just a harsh place to work. Part of our vision was to change that and make the collections team more successful by having them work with the customer base to come up with innovative ways to allow customers to make their payments. Along with many other changes we made, such as training, products, technology, and processes, we also changed the environment.

We put posters of families and our employees in the workplace that said "We help people pay their bills." We painted the place a pale green with white trim and brightened it up. We posted customer letters thanking our people for their help, and we would actually play the "Call of the Month" over the PA system. The change in morale was phenomenal. People began to engage with each other, and there was an upbeat feeling in the call center. You could feel the electricity in the place. The letters from customers, the posters, and playing the calls over the loudspeaker gave us a sense of pride, but more importantly, it reinforced the message that we were there to help customers.

Creativity should be both rewarded and reinforced.

When you begin to change an environment, the momentum of an organization takes over, and the ground swell begins. Soon, everyone is a part of the mission and feeling good about it. Creativity happens because it is sought out and rewarded and reinforced.

In large organizations I have always created a department that manages the environment. Usually I will combine it with human resources, communications, and marketing. In combination, this is an organization that injects momentum and enthusiasm into the organization.

Rewards, recognition, and the physical working conditions all produce the working environment, and having a group or even a committee that manages the activity surrounding the environment will allow you to make tremendous strides in achieving your goals.

Don't Forget the External Environment!

In addition to the internal environment, there is the external environment. In larger organizations, having a community affairs committee that collects money for worthy causes using events such as jeans days, bake sales, picnics, and holiday parties motivates employees when it is done well.

We raised thousands of dollars in our call centers by having jeans days where, for a dollar, you could get a "pass" that would allow you to wear jeans on a weekday when you normally would be required to wear business-casual clothes. We had raffles for major appliances, video games, and baskets around the holidays, and we would donate the money raised to Toys for Tots, having the Marines actually come tour the call center and be presented with the check by an employee. This reinforced our respect and recognition for employees, and it gave us a source of pride as an organization.

When I ran a small department of only seven people, we all joined a Habitat for Humanity program and went into the inner city to build homes. We took pictures, had dinner together, and bonded away from work for a great cause. The following year, we brought our families and some friends, and before long it was our tradition even after the department members had moved on.

All of these things create an atmosphere of a team. They all are aimed at your vision, mission, and values, and most importantly, they make your team a good place to be. Let's face it—you spend a great deal of time at work, and having an environment that is conducive to doing your best is essential. As a manager, you control the environment.

Great managers know that in addition to people, you manage an environment that allows people to achieve great things. You often hear about the "culture" of an organization; the environment is a major part of the culture of the organization. The environment doesn't create a culture; it enables the culture to grow by reinforcing and nurturing it.

An environment is a key ingredient of a successful organization, and most managers do not understand that it's even there. Manage your environment with strategies, execution, and accountability, like you manage everything else. Assign responsibility and watch the energy begin to flow.

Chapter 8

Presentations

- Management Reviews
- Management Asks
- Staff Meetings
- Town Hall
- Speeches

One of the many things you will need to do as a manager is to communicate through making presentations. This management task is frequently met with fear, anxiety, and reservation. Most people are afraid of public speaking; in fact, in a survey I once read that public speaking is people's number-one fear, even more than death! And as the joke goes, that means at a funeral most people prefer being the dead guy to being the one giving the eulogy! But as a manager, if you cannot present, then you are dead! So how do you master the art of presentation?

There are a number of presentation settings, and each will pose different challenges, so it's best to review each type and develop the entire skill set you need to become a great presenter. The most common types of presentations are:

- Management reviews
- Management asks
- Staff meetings
- Town halls
- Speeches

Management Reviews

Your business review presentations should communicate your business results to your management.

There are times in the business cycle when you will have to present your business results to your senior management. The most important thing you need to remember is that your business review presentations have one purpose, and that is to communicate the story of your business results to your management. The presentation itself must tell the story you want to tell your management. So the first thing to ask yourself is what you want to tell your management about your business. Was this a great month? Why did you achieve what you did? What aspects of the business do you need to receive support and continue doing, and what things do you need to change? The presentation should tell the story. Each page should have a takeaway message, perhaps in a bold headline. As the presenter, you need to know what that takeaway message is, and you need to deliver it.

Think of your presentation on your monthly business reviews as writing and then telling a story, because that is exactly what you are doing—telling the story of your performance over the month. The first thing you need to do is meet with your management team and discuss the performance highlights and issues. Out of that discussion should come the key points for the presentation. Having had the discussion, both you and your team have taken a valuable first step toward a great presentation—you are living it!

As you rehearse your discussion, you will play out the conversation as your management review most likely will go—where you identify rough spots in the practice conversation, rest assured they will be the same rough spots in the live review. This may result in you thinking through some alternative approaches to explanations and discussion topics, and it also should result in you changing the presentation somewhat. Add a PowerPoint slide where you need some clarity, put in some backup slides in the appendix, and make other changes that will help you present the materials.

Next, you should have a solid outline of what you want to present and the slides laid out at least in a draft of the presentation. At this point, you need to sit down and write the messages you want to deliver slide by slide. You should do this to whatever level you need to be comfortable—write it out word by word if need be. This is a twofold process: First, you are preparing notes for the presentation, but second and more importantly, you are committing your thought process to memory.

This exercise is not intended to make you memorize what you are going to say—that is different than committing something to memory. For example, if you were to tell me a story about what happened to you last week, you would do it from memory, but you wouldn't have memorized it. You will find the same thing with your preparation. As you exercise for the presentation by making notes on each page, tying in pages, and making backup pages to make a point, you are committing the presentation to memory.

If you've ever heard a presenter say, "We will get to that in a few more pages," or "In a few minutes I am going to take you through some numbers," you know the power of knowing the presentation inside and out. As a speaker, it keeps you in command and allows you to deal with questions and observations with confidence. It does something else as well—it prepares you.

As a manager, you always need to prepare for whatever you are going to present, and the better the preparation, the better the presentation. Having the story and having it well laid out is a big part of being successful as a presenter. But when you are going to speak to your senior management about your results, you need a few more things going for you.

Be prepared! The more prepared you are, the better your presentation will be.

Always, always know your audience.

First, know your audience. That applies no matter who you are talking to, but in the case of senior management discussions, it is a key to survival. Most senior managers like to start out at a high level and discuss the essence of what the topic is, and then they like to either move on or drill deeper. The only way you know that is to read them and pay attention. Your presentation should be written in that manner, and you should present it in that manner to senior management.

When I present, I usual start out with a quick outline or agenda and very quickly run through what the presentation is going to cover. Then I ask, "Is there anything in particular you want us to cover in addition to these topics?" This provides an immediate interaction with the audience on fairly safe ground. It allows you to feel out the audience a bit and get yourself comfortable in the setting.

As you start slide by slide, make your points (takeaways), indicating any of the points on the slides that help make the point and tell the story. For example, you might start with the financials and say, "This month our bottom line was x, driven by the following things a, b, and c." You might follow that with what you think of the driving factors—are you concerned about them, do you have them in control, are they sustainable, are they avoidable, and so on.

The storyline of a particular month may be that you overran expenses, but it is not a trend, and you have taken actions to reverse course. You may want to talk about how this happened, what broke down, how you addressed it, and what to expect going forward.

Even as you read that sentence, you can see that someone who has that command even over a failure is someone you can trust to lead the team out of the problem.

Believe in what you're saying. If you don't, no one else will.

Giving the presentation has one nonnegotiable item for me: You have to believe what you are saying because if you don't, no one else can. Here again, that is why preparation is so important. As you prepare, you get to work the issues or the trends a bit and see what you are comfortable saying and what you are not.

When you have finalized your presentation and made all your notes, you then have one thing to do before you present. Close your office door, clear off your desk, flip through the presentation, and play it out in your mind. What questions will you get and when? What are the toughest questions you might get, and how will you answer them?

I once was in a business review, and I knew that we had a tough month. One of the expense items that was over budget was our sales commissions. It seems that our cost of funds and pricing discounts did serious damage to our revenues. The sales volumes, however, were over budget; hence, the sales commissions were also over what was expected. I opened the presentation with the statement, "This month we learned a painful lesson in managing our financial model. Our variable costs are at a fixed rate, driven by one variable volume, while the remaining variables, such as discounts and operating processing expenses, were driven by volume as well. The lesson here was that our revenues are driven by prices that we monitor daily and set in full control and by funding expenses, which are variable rates not managed by us or factored into our pricing in the same way our costs are. We have corrected that and will move forward."

I anticipated most of the questions I was asked about control and how things were done daily, pricing, funding, and so on. But I thought about it from a standpoint that I hoped would not come up—should we fire someone over this?

As I prepared for that review and thought of that question, I exercised it over and over in my mind. In discussion with my human resources director, she had pointed out that most of the time people get fired for not executing their job in accordance with their defined role, the vision, or the mission or by not abiding by the value system. In this case none of that occurred. Rather, this issue was one of the organization responsibilities not matching the financial model; we had no one whose job it was to monitor funding costs in our pricing area. That was done in accounting at month end; the pricing model had a standard cost built into it for funding that, over time, would even out.

When that question was asked of me in the review, I went through the logic that I had lived and believed in, and it was accepted. If I had not thought about that question, it would have clearly thrown me, and perhaps we would have had a different outcome.

People often ask me, "Where did you come up with that response? It was great!" The fact is, by the time I go to a review, I have been there two or three times in my mind, and everyone else there is going through it for the first time.

Slide by slide, you need to think through what the points will be, what the questions will be, how the discussion might go, what the key things you want to get across are, and how you will go about getting them across.

The reason people are nervous or hesitant about giving presentations is in part that they are giving up control of a situation. However, the more you are prepared, the more you are in control. I once was in a review, and every time my boss would ask me a question, I literally said, "Turn the page." This had happened about six times when my boss finally said to me, "Am I that predictable?" The point is that any boss is in fact that predictable—he or she is going to ask you the same questions you would ask if you were in that position.

One thing you want to do is to commit to and maintain followups during your presentation. There will be times when you do not have the answer, or you may not have the time to get into the explanation. In these cases it is best to simply take a note and commit to getting back to the topic at a subsequent time if that is an acceptable practice.

Always remain steady during a presentation, no matter how well or poorly it goes.

You want to remain even-keeled in a presentation no matter how good or bad it is. This is a chess match in communications: If you are prepared, you know your audience, and you have thought through all the aspects of the presentation, then you are ready to do your job as best as you possibly can, and that is all you ever need be able to do as an employee and as a manager.

Management Asks

There is only one way to get resources: You have to ask!

As a manager, one of your responsibilities will be to ask for resources. This implies that you have assessed the need for the resources and you believe that the investment in the resources you require will best position you and the company to achieve your vision and the mission you have been charged to achieve. In business, resources basically come in two types: money and people. Regardless of the resource you need to achieve your goals, one thing is for certain: You have to ask for it. There are usually committees such as the capital appropriations committee, the technology steering committee, the project management office, the asset liability committee, the finance committee, the human resources committee, the board of directors, the office of the chairman, and various management committees—all designed to hear the case and some designed to make the decision about whether to give the resources to the requestor!

When you need to make a presentation to these groups, the tone is a bit different. You are not telling a story of what happened to the business in the past month or quarter or projecting out where you will take the business going forward. Here, you are making a case of what *could* be. Regardless of the desperation of the situation, the reality of the ask is just that simple—you are making a case of what could be.

The tone, content, and dialogue around this type of presentation is different than a business review. Business reviews, as we discussed, are about the status of the mission. Asking for more resources than you had previously allocated to your business is all about why—why should we allocate or invest more in this business?

Now, if it were a resource ask included in your original plan and mission, then it should be a relatively easy question to answer. The simple answer is, "Because it is time." An example would be if in your original plan you intended to move your organization to a new space to accommodate the expansion of your business. You selected the space, drew up the plans, and now were asking for the resources for which you had already received approval.

In this scenario, you want to answer the why question by briefly revisiting the plan to make sure nothing has changed—or if something has, then you want to be sure that the original proposition and economics still make sense and the timing is still appropriate. If that is the case, then it is really a question of whether the parent company has the resources (namely, money) to continue with the investment in the business.

The factors that impact this ask are business performance versus plan and the company's appetite for investment at that particular junction. As the manager, you control the former directly and contribute (hopefully positively) to the latter. Your presentation needs to be focused on the fact that you have done what you said you were going to do. After all, if you have and it has turned out the way you planned, then this investment should work out as well. If the plan is not on target, then you have to ask yourself the tough question before anyone else does: Why?

Why should your firm continue to invest in this plan if it is not on target? It may be that there was an extraordinary item or issue, and except for that the plan is working. It may be that the plan is working but taking longer than anticipated. Perhaps a strong competitor emerged and is slowing the momentum and success or even threatening it. Regardless of the issue, for your ask to be granted you will need to address the concern head on, in a manner that you and those around you will believe in.

The content and presentation are what ultimately matter.

Factors such as timelines, performance versus plan, refreshed assumptions, new events in the market, and your track record are all key to your successful presentation. Excerpts from your original plan (actual slides are powerful reminders) and an update in bold in a box on the slide are very powerful techniques for presenting, but I am sure you can come up with the format. It is the content and how you present it that will matter in the end.

Here again, preparation is the key to any great presentation. The steps are the same: Outline your ideas, draft slides, discuss with your team, exercise the presentation, discuss questions that may come up, gain a degree of comfort with the material that is unsurpassed, and anticipate the questions, conversations, and outcomes.

Be ready for constituents to have narrow interests limited to their own disciplines.

Also, it really pays to know your audience, because most of these types of sessions are with committees. There is always a finance person, a compliance person, a chief operating officer, a systems head, and others that you will need to address specifically as you make the case for the ask. Each of these constituents has a broad view, but a narrow interest at times limited to his or her discipline. That typically is where you can get derailed, so be ready for that.

I usually craft a message tailored to each of the constituents and make sure I address each one along the way to let them know that I have thought about their concerns and how I am responding to them. That also allows for their participation in a controlled manner. In other words, when you review the finance section, you will get the finance questions. When you review the technology implications, you will field those concerns and questions. It also does one more thing that is very important: It places you in charge of the cadence of the presentation. It allows you to defer questions—"We will get to that in a few pages"—and allows you to remain in control, on track, and more importantly, on point.

Now there is the matter of the ask that is not included in your plan and is new news about your business. Not bad or good news—that really isn't the issue; new news—that's the issue. Remember, all resource managers and gatekeepers need an answer to one question: Why? So all presentations that ask for resources must answer that question, and the faster you can get to that answer, the better off you will be. Have you ever seen a defense attorney or a prosecutor make an opening statement in a case, whether live or on TV? That is a great example of the ask. In his case, the attorney is asking the jury for a verdict, and he begins with something like, "Over the course of this trial, I will prove...." The language changes, but the approach should be the same.

You might start with, "Our business has changed do to x, y, and z over the last few months, and we need to respond to these new changes. Today, I would like to discuss our need for a, b, and c resources as a result of those changes." That simple lead-in will make all the difference. I refer to that statement as the *context statement* that will allow the gatekeepers to begin to think about your need from your perspective and will point them to the reasons for the ask. They will not simply focus on the absolute ask without the context, which is often the case.

In this way, your presentation then serves to reinforce the solution to the dilemma. The dialogue that follows usually has everyone around the table with the same goal—how to successfully deal with the new information and the need that has arisen from it. And if that's the topic, you can only win for your business and yourself.

Regardless of how the ask came about, never personalize it or cause the positioning to be a binary one—namely, win-lose. Always be open to new solutions and be flexible in your style. In the end, these sessions will usually net a good solution if they are collaborative and not arbitrated.

Never dismiss new solutions without considering them.

Staff Meetings

Whether they are presenting to their direct reports at their own staff meeting or they are presenting at their boss's staff meeting, most people do not prepare themselves adequately for such moments. Maybe it is the familiarity of the surroundings or the audience, but over the years I have noticed that this is an area where most managers show up with their B game when the A game is almost always required.

To begin with, as with any speech, you need to think through what you will say, how you will say it, what the audience's reaction will be, and how you will react and adjust. Because a staff meeting is a group of players with dependencies, you need to address the needs you have and the implications your pitch has for them. It is always a good idea to draw on previous experiences with the team if you can to remind them that you have done these things as a team before. Also, what you are asking each of them to do must be clear.

Staff meetings are team oriented, so engage the entire team, not just selected members.

In an information update as well as an ask from a staff meeting setting, you need to share your logic and invite input. In this way, you are engaging the team, and a better outcome will prevail. As a general rule, in staff meetings you should not monopolize the conversation. Pause and ask for input, and avoid talking to just one member or the boss if it is his or her meeting.

I remember my first presentation to my peer group at my boss's staff meeting. I wanted to propose a new process for managing our fixed-asset register. I started the meeting by saying that I had proposed the idea to my boss, and he really liked it and suggested I bring it up at the staff meeting. Strike one: I had just alienated the entire group by basically saying that I went to the boss without them, sold my concept, and this was just an information update with no need for input. I then began to tell them why the current process was flawed and did not work, and how the new process was much better. Strike two: I had just announced that I was the smartest person in the room, and I didn't know how no one had noticed this before me! Thank God for me!

I then handed out a timeline with the dates by which we would need to implement the new process. Strike three: I had not considered that my colleagues might indeed have some things they were doing, such as running a department, that might interfere with my rollout! The bottom line here is that the meeting was a disaster, with all kinds of pushback and issues raised to my fantastic idea, and it took us a few months to get back on track.

My boss's advice to me after the meeting was that I should have pre-sold the idea. This was terrible advice—the fact is, I wasn't selling anything. What I should have done was been more respectful to my colleagues and presented the idea the exact same way I presented it to my boss—as a concept, not a done deal—and sought their input and opinions from the concept to the implementation schedule. That was what the meeting was for in the first place.

Remember, with any concept you are discussing, you have thought about it for a long time, and generally you have worked through the issues in your mind. However, your audience is hearing it for the first time, so you are bound to hear some of the same things you thought about. When you are asked about them, share your logic to test it, if nothing else.

Know whether you are asking for permission, opinion, or support—those are three very different asks—and let people know right up front what the purpose of the presentation is.

If I had started off that meeting with, "Our boss has asked me to implement a new fixed-asset system, and I am here today to explain the new system and ask for your support in implementation," that might have gone much better.

The same thing holds true at your own staff meetings. When you are presenting a concept to your team, they can endorse it because you are the boss, or they can endorse it because they believe in it. To believe in it they have to understand it, and that means they have to remove their doubts through debate and questioning. You need to invite that behavior in your presentation of such concepts.

When you present a concept, invite people to debate and question to gain understanding of the concept.

You need to state the purpose of the discussion right up front. Why are you presenting something to your staff? Is it informational? Is it requesting their support or approval? Then tailor the discussion toward the objective.

I once reorganized our division, and I called a staff meeting to announce it. I started out by saying that I'd had several one-on-one meetings with the staff, human resources, my boss, and some key members of his management team and reached a conclusion on how best we should organize. I further stated that the purpose of this meeting was to communicate my final decision on our organizational structure. It was pretty clear that this wasn't about input or opinion—I had decided something, and I wanted their support.

If you can sort out the ask in any meeting (but particularly your staff meetings), you will be amazed at the alignment of the group. The particular challenge of the staff meeting is that it is such an open-ended meeting as to its purpose that the objectives of the meeting are not always clearly defined or communicated.

Town Hall

Anyone who knows me knows that this is one of my favorite presentation settings—the town hall! This meeting is all about preparation; the better you can prepare yourself here, the better your meeting will be. Town halls are all about information—what is being communicated, how it is being communicated, and how it is being received. The truth is that you control almost all of that.

> You cannot run a successful town hall unless you know what people want to talk about.

To begin with, to run a successful town hall, you need to know what people want to talk about. The best way to find out is to ask them point blank. A week before my town halls, I always send out an email to the population at large, directing them to an anonymous mailbox with topics and/or questions for the town hall. I then build my town hall in three parts.

1. What do I want to talk to people about?
2. What do people want me to talk to them about?
3. What is our performance against our goals?

Essentially, that is any town hall.

What do you want to talk to people about? There are certain things that you and/or your management team want to talk about to your employees—a new program; a benefit signup; the vision, mission, and values of the company; particular problems or issues you are facing; the external or internal environment; good things that are happening; failures you want to address; systemic issues...the list goes on and on. But these are issues you want to speak to your employees about, and they are what you should lead off your town hall meetings with.

From your survey you conduct the week before, you will get topics to incorporate into your presentation as well, and you will get questions that you should treat as write-in questions for your floor question-and-answer session. This allows you to cover the topics in a logical and thorough fashion and to be prepared for the communication in a way you simply cannot always be from the podium or the floor.

Be honest and open with the ad hoc questions and answers. Remember, you don't always have to have the answer, but you *do* always have to commit to getting the answer and following up.

Employees like to hear a leader who speaks their language as well as the executive mumbo jumbo, so mix it up a bit. I once was asked if I thought we paid people fairly. I simply said yes. Then I paused and said, "Now, how do you suppose I know that?" I then proceeded to discuss our salary surveys, our compensation committee's work, and our recruiting efforts, all as data points that told me our compensation structure was in line with the market. But it was the yes and the pause that people remembered most—they soon forgot how I knew the pay was fair, but they knew we went through a big effort to ensure they were paid fairly.

Someone once asked me if I would do a deal we had done again. The deal was a disaster and had all sorts of ramifications. I simply said "No, that was a mistake; we need to learn from it and move on." Simple, to the point, and with no need for any further discussion. People appreciate honesty and clarity more than you know. Frankly, the mistake executives often make is that they talk too much, and they defend too much. Town halls are not job interviews or quizzes; they are open and honest discussions about how you and your employee base feel about things.

> Honesty and clarity from a manager are always appreciated.

No town hall should happen without a discussion about the business's performance. It is your chance as a leader to point to the scoreboard and let the team know how they are doing—good or bad. The most important thing to let them know is why—why is the performance the way it is, and how can they improve it to the next level? People always want to know where the company stands, where they stand, and how to do better, and there is no better place than the town hall to tell them.

Keep your slides very simple in a town hall. Remember the size of the group: The larger the group, the larger the white space on the slides! Pictures and graphics versus words and bullet points—this is about you talking to them and them talking to you. The presentation here is simply for context.

Remember: What you think about you talk about, and what you talk about you bring about. The town hall is a time to talk about the things you want to bring about.

Speeches

I could write another book on how to give speeches that would amass hundreds of pages, but here are a few key points, some of which we discussed previously but are worth repeating.

Know your audience! Not long ago, at a management meeting I attended a session entitled "Getting the Most out of Your Employees." It was an internal training for senior managers, except the instructor did not realize the experience or level of the people in the room. She began to tell the group of executives—who each, by the way, managed a country (I had the U.S.)—how we should walk around and be visible to our people on a daily basis. My colleague who managed Russia, where he had more than 50 storefronts, and was officed in the U.K. asked, "What if that is logistically impossible?" Her response was that if he were committed to being a better manager, he would find a way. On the break, I told her it might be a good idea if she knew what we did for a living before she continued.

I spoke to a group of sales employees for a top pharmaceutical company about being an A performer. Part of my speech covered the fact that one of the reasons why salespeople are driven as hard as they are is because they only get paid if they make a sale, and the rewards are typically very generous because they are the revenue generators. Nice touch, huh? Well, this sales force was 75-percent salaried and had a cap on their bonuses. Luckily, I got out backstage before the revolt took place!

Don't forget about the audience: Tailor your presentation to them!

It's really quite simple: You need to do some research on your audience and tailor your message to them. The more you can align what you have to say to fit the people you are speaking to, the better you will connect.

Also, read your audience. If they are laidback and casual, you may want to give a more comfortable delivery. If they are energetic, then you need to feed that energy.

Before you speak to a group, it is a good idea to research what the group is all about. Speak to some of the leaders—not just the CEO, but a few leaders—and if you can visit the place or use the product, do so to increase your frame of reference so you can tie in your comments directly to the people.

Humor can be useful...to a point.

Humor is good to a point, but when you become a comedian, you've gone too far. One joke or two is great, depending upon the reaction you receive. Remember, what is funny to you may not be funny to the audience, so here again research is a key. If you can observe or interact with your crowd beforehand, it's simple—walk around the first few rows and just introduce yourself. Shake a few hands and get a feel for what they want to hear, how the event is going so far, and so on.

Be an observer and take in the crowd as much as you can. Even from the stage, you can see the body language. Engage them if you can—point out someone who is laughing, someone who is nodding, and so on. This brings a feeling of interaction that is otherwise lacking in most speeches.

Be humble but confident, and most of all, be yourself. Usually the day before I speak, I take the time to go over my speech in my head. I visualize the appearance as much as I can. If it is an hour-long talk, I go through it from beginning to end, working on the transitions, the timing, and the delivery. Trust me: The effort you put into preparation will pay off in your delivery.

Be yourself!

Chapter 9

Expense Management

- Plan Your Expenses
- Understand Drivers
- Assess Your Performance
- Make Adjustments
- Measure

Any time you talk about a successful manager, one of the things that invariably comes up is how well (or not so well) he or she manages expenses. Regardless of the size of the budget that you manage, the approach, responsibility, and accountability are the same. This is a fact that often escapes managers—particularly managers in large organizations.

A cost center budget is essentially the same as a personal budget in many ways.

Your cost center budget is no different than your personal budget in many respects, but managers often feel that there is this source of money in business that allows them to overrun the budget with no penalty. In fact, most do early in their career and have reinforced for them that a budget overrun is no big deal, until they are in a large-scale position and get themselves in trouble to the point of a failure.

I remember a business review where the division head was told by one of my colleagues that he expected to be over budget by 20 to 25 percent. His reasoning was that he had miscalculated the cost of a major project because the effort to complete the project was greater than anyone had envisioned. The division head simply looked at him and said, "So where do you think the money will come from to pay for this?" My colleague was dumbfounded and replied, "I don't know." Now imagine if this were his personal budget, and he planned an expenditure that he could not afford to pay. What would have happened to him? Bankruptcy, wage garnishment, lawsuit...the list goes on and on and is ever more painful.

Yet when confronted with the same dilemma in business, we think that somehow it's all going to be okay. But if every manager managed in this manner, the company would wind up facing the same situation as in a personal budget dilemma. This is a fact that many do not see very clearly, but those who can manage expenses and deliver on their performance often gain greater responsibility and success.

If you can manage expenses and deliver, you are likely to earn greater responsibility and success.

So why is expense management one of those managerial responsibilities that is often problematic? It's simple, really: Most managers do not see the money being spent until it is spent, and by then it's too late. At the beginning of every year is the budget exercise where a company determines how much money it plans on spending and what they will get in return for the expenditures. This exercise generally produces a cost center expense budget that the manager is responsible for throughout the year. It's the first step in a management process that allows one to manage his or her expenses.

Then as the year unfolds, you begin to track your performance versus that plan to see where you are and how well you are getting the job done at the expense levels the company wants to spend. Where you are off plan, higher or lower, you need to make adjustments, and where you are on plan, you need to determine whether the value being extracted is what you thought for that level of expenditure and make adjustments there as well.

Most unsuccessful managers often are too late to assess their position and then too slow to make the adjustments, if they make them at all. So, how does this work and how will you become the best expense manager you could be?

Let's start with the process to manage expenses:

1. Plan your expenses.

2. Understand drivers.

3. Assess your performance.

4. Make adjustments.

5. Measure.

These are the five sacred rules of expense management, and you need to run through these steps each month to ensure that you are managing your expense base to its optimal performance.

Plan Your Expenses

Seems pretty simple, doesn't it? You run a department, and you anticipate the activity you will have in that department and how much money you will need to perform that activity. All true, but you also need to predict the outcome of that activity—in other words, what will it produce. That is where managers often go wrong. When the managers are not getting the results they need, they begin to change the plan—and when they do, one of the things that changes is the cost of the activity. That is where they most often get burned in the process.

A change of plan results in a change in the cost of an activity.

Imagine you run a small department of 10 people, and you need to produce 10 widgets each day. You plan on each person producing a widget each day, and the year begins. One thing you notice after the first month of work is that you are only producing 9 widgets per day, so instead of having 200 widgets (20 work days times 10 widgets per day) at the end of the month, you only have 180. Your supervisor has a great idea; he can bring in some part-time help—two people who can produce the remaining 20 widgets needed to meet your goal. You like the idea and agree. Sure enough, the second month you have 200 widgets right on the nose! Success? Not at all, because you had planned to produce widgets at a cost of 10 people per 200, and now you are producing them at a cost of 10 people plus 2 part-time people. This is an expense management fail, and you will now have less of a margin and less of a profit as a result.

Great expense managers are managing an expense plan, not expenses.

That seems pretty basic, but I can tell you that not many people understand this example in real-life application. I was asked to run an organization that was struggling with delivering a certain product on time. The managers and I met, and they told me one of the largest issues they had was with one of the vendors they were using. They had planned a certain productivity level for this vendor, and the vendor was not meeting it, causing them to fall behind schedule. Their solution was to replace the vendor with a new vendor that had finished second in the initial project bid. They had done due diligence on the second vendor with references, and they were very confident that the new vendor was the solution to the problem.

When I asked, "What is the difference between the new vendor's cost and the existing one?" I was surprised at the response. The managers told me it really didn't matter because we had to get this product out to meet the organization's plan! I smiled and said, "Do we not have an expense plan as well?" Those managers' mentality is one that often leads to expense overruns and deteriorated profit margins. The fact is we had planned for a certain outcome, and we were not achieving the outcome. The flaw was the vendor choice, and now that we had some experience, we knew our plan was wrong: We could not get the results at the planned level of expenditure.

So, if this were your personal budget, what would you have to do? You could borrow money and change vendors, which would certainly reduce your bank account. If that were acceptable to you, that might be a good decision. Alternatively, you could choose the new vendor, reexamine all other costs, and reduce spending in some other areas so that the full expenditure was still the same number. But what you cannot do is simply incur more costs without discussion and alignment of goals and continue on your way.

Think about expense management in terms of how much money you have, how much you plan to spend, and the gap between those two. Your role as a manager is to minimize that gap without deteriorating the business.

I had a department that had terrible customer service levels. These levels were driven by the fact that a scheduled systems enhancement had been delayed by several months. The enhancement would eliminate about 30 jobs in customer research, and people had left the company. The manager did not want to replace the people, because the system enhancement would eliminate jobs. The net result was that the department was severely understaffed for the workload, and customer service had deteriorated rapidly.

When I walked into the manager's office to meet her, I couldn't help but notice five framed certificates on her office wall. Her department had performed the best on expense management versus the plan for the first five months of the year, and she was awarded a certificate each month for expense management! This is the other side of the issue. Expense management is the amount of money you plan on spending to produce a certain outcome or return. In this case, the manager was spending less money than she planned, but she was getting far worse results than she planned as well. Most companies look at the variables one at a time, which is why expense management is such a lost art these days.

> Expense management: the amount of money you plan to spend to produce a certain outcome or return.

Not only was this manager running the place into the ground on service levels, she was being rewarded! Any variance to a plan needs to be reviewed in the context of the plan, not as an absolute or isolated variable. Remember, great expense managers are managing an expense plan, not expenses.

Understand Drivers

There are certain activities that will drive your expenses on a continued basis, day after day, month after month. You need to identify these drivers and understand their behaviors by tracking them and analyzing them.

> You must identify which activities will drive your expenses on a continued basis.

Each year I plan my personal budget. When I first began this process, I remember asking my gas company how much it would cost to heat my house, because it was my first house, and I had no idea. In fact, I was really clueless because I had come from a poor family, and we seldom had heat in the winter!

The gas company, being the good sports they are, told me that a house the size of mine should cost about $50 per month. It was April when I moved into that house in New Jersey, a very nice time of year. I allocated my $50 per month out of my paycheck and was pleasantly surprised that my first three bills were about $30. To a newly married couple struggling with the expenses of a house, this was great news—and it continued right up until October, when I noticed our bill went to $45. Then $60 in November, $75 in December, and $100 in January! You can imagine my panic. I thought to myself, "This could reach $1,000 at this pace!"

Of course it didn't. New Jersey began to get warmer in March, and then April, and so on. But what exactly happened here? My heating bill was budgeted in a straight line, which was not how the expense flowed in, so I never really knew where I stood until it was too late (after I incurred the expense). In addition, I did not understand the driver here being the weather.

You must plan expenses the way they are incurred.

I learned two things that winter that had never occurred to me, despite having a 4.0 in accounting and a 3.7 in economics from one of the best universities on the East Coast. I learned that expenses must be planned the way they are incurred, and I learned that one must understand the drivers of expenses to accurately predict and control them.

First you have to identify the largest expenditures in your plan. Often in today's management environment, that is people, but there are many others, too. Once you define them, you need to predict their behaviors—what will be the frequency, velocity, and predictability? Next, you need to set indicators that tell you the progression line of expenses. So if you were managing people costs, you would look at salaries, overtime, and benefits, and your indicators might be overtime hours, number of people in each area, and benefits cost per person. You then can track these by reviewing your turnover, new hires, open requisitions, monthly benefit payments, and other indicators that will help you understand and, more importantly, control the variables.

Once you identify, define, and track expenditures, you can begin to control expense tradeoffs.

You then can begin to control the expense tradeoffs. My wife and I wore blankets while we watched TV, instead of turning up the thermostat. The blankets were about a $15 one-time expenditure for both of us, and we lowered the heating bill by $15 per month! We also turned down the heat during the day when we were not home. Suddenly, we became heat consumption experts, as we began to understand the behavior of the expense and the drivers that led to alternative cost-effective solutions—also known as blankets!

Drivers are not always obvious to the process. When I ran an operating center, one of my largest expenses was in a category called discretionary write-offs. Here, if we could not balance out on our financial transactions, we would write off up to $150 on each transaction. When I asked why, people told me that a Six Sigma study years before revealed that it cost us about $150 per transaction to research and resolve these out-of-balance situations; therefore, it made better economic sense to simple write off the amount than to spend more to resolve it than it was literally worth.

Because the expense item was a big one, we wrote off about 100 a month. That was $180,000 a year, and my entire budget was about $6,000,000, so I was giving away 3 percent (which happened to be my raise or merit pool to this process). So, I decided to look into what drove this expense.

Here's what I found out: When we had a balance in a transaction, it generally was because of one of four issues:

A. The customer short paid.

B. We billed incorrectly.

C. A vendor overcharged us.

D. We made a reconciliation error, meaning we had the cash and just didn't know where it was.

I decided to take a month's worth of data and see which of the four areas was the largest cause. My staff, who had been there through the Six Sigma process, kept telling me, "We did this already," and I kept telling them, "Good, so you know the process." Well, the study turned out to be fairly accurate three years later, and we were writing off roughly the same amount in each of the categories.

Understanding the driver of an expense is the first step in reducing it.

The interesting piece of data that I saw was this: In the area where we billed the customer incorrectly, Category B, the majority of the errors took place where we had not billed an application fee. The rules around billing the application fee were a bit complex. By law, we could not profit on an application for credit, where the funds we collected were simply used to pay a vendor to perform a service to perfect the credit. So, when we used a credit vendor, that piece of the application fee was a pass-through fee, but we didn't always use it. If you understand this, congratulations—I had people who worked for me for 10 years who never understood what I just wrote, and this was their business!

I suggested that we actually split this out on our fee schedule as a separate line item, and after arguing it with the sales force (who didn't want to sell another fee), we did just that.

The results amazed me. The month after we began, my write-offs dropped to $100,000, and we settled out at about $75,000. We actually solved for two of the four categories with this fix—the vendor billings and the customer billings going out incorrectly or short billed. I am not saying the Six Sigma process didn't work—it did. We just Six Sigma'd the wrong thing! Understanding the driver of an expense is the first step in reducing it.

Assess Your Performance

Expense management is about what you get for what you spend. Now, before you tell me that my statement is no revelation, stop a moment and think about the last time a manager asked you what you received for the amount of money you spent. This basic concept is lost in today's corporate world. Most expense management is about what you spend, period, and therein lies the problem. Whether you are an auto parts purchaser or the CEO of the auto company, you need to understand, monitor, and examine the input and output of expense management.

In 1999 I ran a fairly large-scale operation with three operating centers throughout the country. We were constantly sending documents back and forth through the centers and to customers. We were in the mortgage business, and there is no more paper-intense business in existence. So you can imagine the opportunity we saw when we examined imaging solutions. As every good management team would do, we had studied it, worked it out, analyzed it, and met on it for about eight months, and we were ready to roll it out in two weeks!

The problem with most expense management is that it is only about what you spend, not what you receive in return.

Actually, the rollout went well, and we "booked the save," as they say. The savings would come from our overnight delivery charges, because we would image documents so each center would have access to them electronically and we would not incur the overnight shipping—at least that was the plan. Having declared success, the management team went on to the next dragon to slay. After about two months, my CFO came storming into my office one morning with the news that our shipping bill did not go down—actually, it didn't even change. Not a penny!

Impossible! We installed the imaging solution, the technology department assured me that people were using the technology—they can track that stuff, you know—all the procedures were updated, and policies were issued, so what was the problem? Well, first, we took the easy way out—there were some backlogged bills, burn in, accrual reversals, and so on. That must be it! But another month went by, and still no reduced shipping costs.

So, I did what any good leader does when faced with a question he or she is not getting an answer to: I increased the population that I was asking. Sure enough, it worked. In a focus group at one of those three centers, I mentioned that we put in the imaging solution and everyone was using it and seemed to like it a great deal, but we were still not seeing any shipping cost reduction, and I wondered why. Wonder no more—one of the clerks looked me right in the eye and said, "That's because we still have to ship the files." What? Why would we still have to ship the files?

It turned out that the fraud department needed to see original documents to properly assess the potential fraudulent activity. Of course, we never thought of centralizing the fraud department, which we now could easily do since all the documents were coming to the image center!

Assessing the performance of an expense management initiative to ensure that the input and output get the desired impact is critical because expenses are just a result of activity, and expense management is activity management.

The key measurement is efficiency ratio: The dollar you spend on expenses produces how much revenue (or savings to expense)? When I was at one of the largest banks in the nation, we had a classic example of the impact of the lack of this metric. It was B.P. (Before PowerPoint), when one used foils projected on an overhead projector on a conference-room wall to make a presentation. There was a major expense initiative at that time (in the late '80s and early '90s), and the expense authorities decided that we could save paper if we did away with handouts. This is similar to today's environmentally sound suggestion to double-side presentations. Yes, that is always the first thing the expense

The key to assessing expense management performance is efficiency ratio.

czar suggests—the old double-sided-paper routine. It sounds good—environmentally friendly or, as we say today, green—but it's absolutely worthless and never works out. But I digress—in this story, the suggestion was even better than the old double-sided one. It was no more paper, and no more handouts period!

Now imagine 22 executives at a business review, and all you have to go on to review the business are these cloudy foils that you can barely see! Not to mention that you could no longer send your presentation to the audience so they could familiarize themselves with it, analyze it, ask the pointed value-added questions, refer to it the next month, or even hand it off for follow-up and better communications.

We not only lost productivity in meetings, lost valuable advice and insight from senior leaders, and ran the business sub-optimally because we no longer had the information, we didn't save much because people made bootleg copies—sent presentations out to Kinko's so no one could track the copy count and charge them penalties!

You really have to assess the performance you are creating when you engage in expense management—it is a critical key to success.

On the flip side, having an expense plan and understanding the drivers of your expenses will allow you to properly track and assess your performance and reduce expenses without reducing performance, which is true efficiency.

Having an expense plan and understanding the drivers will allow you to reduce expenses without negatively impacting performance.

We had a travel policy that demanded people book the lowest available fare when they traveled. Not a bad idea on the surface—we placed controls with the travel agents that ensured our folks would always book the lowest fare available. Again, after a few months we assessed the performance of the policy. We had a good plan to reduce travel expenses, we understood the main driver—airfares—and we did research that identified we were not booking the lowest fares. Two for two on this endeavor: The expense did not go down. When we assessed the performance, we found out a few things we didn't know going in.

First, the lowest fares were typically the ones you booked furthest in advance. Second, the lowest fares carried a cancellation fee with them, and we cancelled flights—boy, did we ever cancel flights! We would book a meeting, change the date, rebook the meeting, change the date again, and rebook the meeting again!

The administrative assistants figured out how to avoid penalties and still book the lowest *available* fare—book at the last minute. Of course, these were the highest fares of all, but indeed they were the lowest fares available at the last minute, and generally they avoided the cancellation fee!

So, we thought we knew the driver, but we were measuring expenses, not behaviors and activity. Once we realized that the driver was our behavior, the solution to lower airfares had little to do with the plane ticket and everything to do with behavior. We changed when we required face-to-face meetings, and when we did, we required one week's notice and committed to not cancelling. After a painful while, we actually adhered to our new behaviors, and yes, this change combined with the booking of the lowest fares available, which now we actually could do, resulted in our travel expenses decreasing.

Make Adjustments

Nothing is finite in life except perhaps death. Clearly, then, expense management is not finite! Every expense management initiative you undertake needs to be periodically revisited, with adjustments made along the way. I actually learned this fact as I watched the company I was with in the '90s decide to buy a system to replace one we had been outsourcing because the cost of the outsource was simply too high. The service was great, and we were satisfied with the system capability and support—it was just that the cost had been increasingly difficult to manage over the years and had reached a point of diminishing returns. We did a complete analysis, reviewed it with all levels of management, and came to the conclusion that we would convert some modules, build some, buy some others, and *still* be more cost effective and have more control over the long run of our expenses.

> You must periodically revisit and adjust every expense management initiative you undertake.

In fact, when we told the vendor, they agreed to help us do the conversion and supply (at a price) expertise and labor to help us be successful. The project began! It was a two-year effort, and about a third of the way into it, something interesting happened. The vendor was sold to a third party. Instead of continuing on with the effort, I decided to meet with the third party and discuss the pricing one more time. In the discussion, I learned that the new vendor was very interested in keeping us as a client and had ideas about how to improve its internal processes and cost structure and reduce our costs as a result. With this new information we adjusted our position accordingly, and in doing so we insisted that the new vendor do things in such a manner that if we ever decided to move on, we could do it with less effort and risk than with the current way we had our relationship structured.

Expense management is like everything else around it, constantly moving and changing, yet we all think of it as finite, and sometimes we get caught implementing yesterday's idea without the benefit of today's knowledge.

Don't get caught implementing yesterday's idea without the benefit of today's knowledge.

As you have seen in this chapter, you also have to make adjustments based on what you learn in the thought process of expense management. Shifts in process, organizations, and policies, and in people's behaviors often go hand in hand with expense management. In fact, often these related changes make the expense initiatives work.

Expense management is management first and foremost, but we get sidetracked around the emotion of expense management and its potential negative impact on morale. Or we, as managers, are so focused on it that we take a myopic approach to it. But that said, expense management is behavior change, and that is difficult and requires help, motivation, and supervision. In the '90s I worked for a company that was terrible at expense management—in reality it was terrible at management *period;* expense was just a readily measurable form of a task they needed to manage.

Managers would threaten harsh actions if expenses did not decrease, and our CFO would say things like, "We will use blunt instruments if we need to." It would actually be funny if it wasn't sad. Expense management requires a disciplined approach and is often a focus after it's too late, meaning expenses are out of control (in other words, growing faster than revenues). Of course, people often see the "takeaways" but not the benefits. So as a manager, you must tie the two together and connect the dots for them.

You must use a disciplined approach to expense management.

When I was a CFO in an organization that never met a dollar it didn't spend, you can imagine the issues I had to deal with as we began to pick the low-hanging fruit. I recall a suggestion that we take away all the plants in the building. We had a large building, about 400,000 square feet, and boy, did we ever have plants! Our maintenance bill for care and feeding of our plants was about $250,000 per year—all for office plants. As I put this on the list of soon-to-be-implemented expense cuts, my head of human resources suggested that we allow departments to "adopt their plants." She later changed my expense cut list to "smart expense initiatives." She clearly was a master at getting people pointed in the right direction by paying close attention to the way they communicated.

The result was that instead of the hallway chatter being, "They took away our plants," it was a friendly competition among departments on raising their plants. They named their plants, decorated them for the holidays—we spent nothing on them, and the place never looked better! No morale damage, and a $250,000 reduction in expenses. I will say it again: Expense management is just a form of management. Recognizing all the aspects and making the correct adjustments to the environment is part of any management process, but it is often overlooked in expense management.

Sometimes you do need a jumpstart to expense management, and often that means getting a group together (or even committees)—which is fine, but proceed with caution.

The golden rule of expense management is that the person who manages the expense must be accountable for it. Often we create committees that "own" expense lines. My question about this practice is what, then, does the manager of the area own if a committee owns his or her expenses? Committees, task forces, "bullet trains," and so on work well when they make recommendations to a manager who can adopt or not adopt them. They never, never, ever work (got that??) when the committee owns the expenses. The committee can advise, recommend, and even govern and report out on expense management, but not own it. You see, a committee is not held accountable the way a line manager is, and that is for good reason. They are not assigned a cost center or a division to manage day to day, so if a committee suggestion doesn't work out we usually simply eliminate the committee, but if a manager misses a goal, then he or she usually has some type of accountability for it, such as compensation or performance rating. In short, we do not performance-manage committees, we performance-manage people, and that creates accountability.

So form a committee to study expenses, review and gather information on expenses, make recommendations on reducing expenses, and even review and track progress each week, month, or quarter, but not to manage—that is the manager's role.

The person who manages the expense must be accountable for it.

Measure

The Meola rule of management: If it moves, measure it!

The cardinal rule of management is that you cannot manage what you don't measure. That is right up there with the Meola rule of management, which is if it moves, measure it! As you develop your expense management process, you need to set expectations that will be brought about by you managing expenses and then measure yourself against those expectations—constantly adjusting, learning, improving, and reducing your expense base.

Start with what you can measure, and out of that will come new things to measure. Eventually, you will get to the critical expense drivers and control them by measuring them, discussing them, and managing them.

My management team in the early '90s began the simple task of reporting out the average expense on an expense report by area as a way to begin to understand our travel and entertainment expenses. Here is what the report looked like:

Sales	$150
Operations	$100
Marketing	$126
Human Resources	$75
Accounting	$72
Technology	$1,289
Training	$350

What do you notice here? Here was what I noticed: Technology and training looked to be perhaps a bit above the norm—and what the heck is going on in technology, anyway?

Turns out that when our help desk needed a part, they would send a tech over to the local computer store, and he or she would simply buy it because it was much faster than using the Purchasing department's process. That led to another interesting discovery: We were replacing our wireless cards on a regular basis about two or three months after we were buying them—or so we thought. Turns out that we were using a new "cheaper" supplier, and the cards we purchased (about 1,500) were faulty.

If the technology people had used their own process, they would have looked at the purchase and repair expense lines and seen a trend, but since they expensed these to travel and entertainment rather than using the process we had in place, it went undetected until we started measuring the travel and entertainment line. Oh, and the folks in Marketing evidently had a wine connoisseur in the group who enjoyed showing her talents on the company's dime—that was an easy fix.

But none of this would ever have come to light without measuring the expense base. Not only do you need to provide managers with measurements, but a basis benchmark of comparison is required. There is the customary actual versus budget, which is commonly found in good organizations, but in great organizations you will see peer comparisons, improvement ratios versus previous time period, industry best-in-class benchmarks, or other metrics that simply drive one to look at the expenses in terms they otherwise would not see.

If you planned incorrectly up or down and you have met the planned target, what have you really accomplished? That is the problem with the single view versus the plan. If all you looked at was the improvement ratio, and you were above or below average to begin with, what picture does that paint? If you are the best in the company but the worst in the industry for your expenses, what good is looking at the company span over a line of expenses?

The short answer is that the more views you have and the wider the lens, the better you will see and succeed at expense management. More than that, remember that expense management is just management, period!

Chapter 10

Some Final Advice

- ■ Stay Positive
- ■ Think about It
- ■ Be Relentless
- ■ Know When to Engage

Always remember that it is a privilege to manage people.

Being a manager is a great responsibility, and if you remember nothing else, remember that and let it guide you every day. It is a privilege to manage people—you are their role model, their leader, and their advisor. Too many managers—especially new managers—think that when they make it to a supervisor or manager role, it is the top of the mountain. If you take the organizational chart and turn it upside down, you get a much clearer picture of what a manager's role is all about. You are there to produce the optimal result for the company, your people, and ultimately, if you do those two things, yourself!

You must know what the desired result is in order to produce it.

Managing is about results, and you cannot produce the desired result if you do not know what it is. That is why you need a vision and a mission. Since by definition no manager is without people, you need to lead people to that vision by *doing* that mission, and that is why you need values. Values create an environment, and people want to work in an environment that they feel good about and that they can excel in. Your job is to create, develop, and at times protect that environment.

When that environment is right, it will create energy for your people, but more importantly it will create energy for you—energy and excitement, accomplishment and success, and actually fun! You will begin to enjoy what you do in a way you never have experienced before. That's what happens when you are successful. When I lived in Chicago, the Chicago Bulls were one of the best basketball teams ever to take the court—it was the Jordan era. At that same time, I became friends with one of the greatest basketball legends ever to play the game—he was a competitor of the Bulls. When I asked him what made the Bulls so great, he told me an interesting story.

He told me the Bulls clearly had great talent, but they worked harder than any team in the league. Their practice sessions were often long and very engaged, and they were a very selfless group who valued teamwork and executed to perfection. They were smart, and they played smart. But the thing that really struck fear in the opponent was this: They enjoyed playing the game. No matter what the situation, they were having fun. The reason was that they were prepared, they were talented, and they were a team, and the confidence that came from that combination of attributes allowed them to enjoy the game regardless of the situation.

That is management at its best.

Often people ask me what things have allowed me to obtain the success that I have enjoyed in my career as a manager. As I look back on a fairly good run, I would have to say that a few key factors in my life have made all the difference.

Stay Positive

The attitude you bring into the world every morning is about the only thing that you really control in life. My mother used to tell me you cannot always control what happens to you, but you can always control how you react to it—words of wisdom to manage by and perhaps to live by.

"Staying positive" is a misunderstood term. It doesn't mean that you pretend to be happy when you are not, or you ignore bad things or challenging issues. That is a formula for disaster. Staying positive means that whatever situation you are in and whatever circumstances arise, you are ready for them, you rely on yourself to get through in the best way possible, and you enjoy the fact that you can make a difference. Envision the outcome you want to achieve, be realistic about it, and go for it—that is why you are a manager. Someone sees something in you that tells them you are ready to be entrusted with people's lives and business challenges and that you are ready to achieve great things—otherwise, you wouldn't be a manager. Enjoy that fact, develop that spark, and become what others see you can become.

> You can't always control what happens to you, but you can always control how you react to it.

I had to close down an operation in 1991, and in that process we had to lay off more than 1,000 people. On the plane ride back from headquarters, where the decision had been made and communicated to me and my head of human resources, I began to think about the task that was ahead of us. I thought of how we had run the division up until that point, the fact that the market had dealt us a fatal blow, and how the next few weeks would go down.

I decided that we would go through this process the same way we went through everything else—we would have a plan, we would have goals, and we would communicate every step of the way. We would engage our people in solutions, and we would execute flawlessly.

When I stood in front of about 900 people and announced the company's plan and direction, I also announced a plan to help all 900 go through this and come out successful. I used the same words I had in the past about needing them to execute and work together as a team and achieve success. I committed to them that I would do my best for each of them and that I expected they would to their best for each other and for the company.

The result to this day remains as one of my greatest accomplishments. We minimized the pain and anguish of the layoffs; we placed 61 percent of the people by working aggressively with our outplacement firms before the layoffs were completed and an additional 10 percent after the layoffs were done. People sent me cards and letters of thanks, and spouses sent me letters of thanks as well.

We had weekly communications and meetings, we had plans, and we "managed" the layoffs. Frankly, there were times when we had fun during that period. We'd laugh and joke—we took one of the toughest challenges we ever had, and we controlled it because we *could*. I remember at the town hall asking the question that many people reminded me of: "I'd like a show of hands—how many people here worked somewhere else before this company or know someone who works somewhere else other than this company?" When everyone's hand went up, it was followed by laughter and a subliminal recognition that the world had not ended, and we could get through this challenge as well.

That is what I mean about staying positive. I learned the corollary as a young basketball player in high school. I was about 5'7" tall, and I had no business playing high school basketball. I was assigned to cover a high-scoring guard on the opposing team, and my brother gave me some advice before the game began. "Get in his head, trash-talk him to death, get him angry, and that will knock him off his game."

Say what you may about that advice, but what he was really saying was that I should put the kid in a negative mood, and he would not be able to perform. That is exactly what I did, and it worked exactly the way my brother said it would. When you have a negative mood or disposition, you do not think. Notice I didn't say "think properly" or "think straight," I said "think"—as in think at all! The more negative you are the worse you are—that's why teams fall into a tailspin, where nothing seems to go right for them.

That kid I covered was so intently focused on me that he didn't think about the game, scoring, or anything else. He was the best player out there for certain, but that day he couldn't stand on a pier and throw the basketball into the ocean—he'd miss!

As a manager, there will be times when you lose your edge and go negative—after all, you are human. What great managers do is learn to deal with negativity. I don't mean accept it—I mean deal with it. When I "go negative," I close my door and write down the things that are bothering me at that moment. Oddly enough, sometimes when I do that, I write down things that have nothing to do with the moment or even work, but that are weighing me down. I then think about how long these things will last and how I can deal with them in a way that will get me through them.

I cancel calls and meetings and try not to deal with anyone for about an hour, then I go for a walk. My objective is simply to see people—the people I lead, the people in other areas. They're the reason I am a manager in the first place, because all these people rely on me. It makes me feel like I need to answer the call, and frankly, I do just that. Now this may or may not work for you, but the point is that something will. It will change your attitude and give you back control of your situation, but it is a learned behavior, hence you need to discover it for yourself and learn how to deal with it.

Staying positive will also engage help naturally for you. People want to be around positive people and want to be on their team and lend them support. They draw energy from them, and energy makes the environment positive as well.

Remember, staying positive is a mindset, so you cannot fake it. When you are feeling good and having a good day, take a minute to understand why. That will allow you to create a good day by re-creating the things that make a good day. What you will find in this process are the words of Mrs. Meola: It's not so much what happens to you, but rather how you react to it that makes the difference.

> The more negative you are, the worse you perform.

> You cannot fake staying positive.

Think about It

Recently I was watching a pro football playoff game. It was a very close game—your typical fourth-quarter nail biter. The team with the ball was losing by six points, and there was very little time left in the game. It was first down and the clock had stopped, so it was a calm moment in an otherwise hurried game. The quarterback approached the line of scrimmage, adjusting his shoulder pads and swiveling his head to survey the defense. Just before the snap of the ball, the defense rushed toward the line, and as the snap occurred, they blitzed the quarterback! The quarterback instantly threw the ball without hesitation, seemingly to no one—high and off to the right. Out of nowhere, the wide receiver showed up, caught the ball, raced untouched to the end zone—and the team won the game. After the game the quarterback was interviewed about the play. "I had thought about that situation all week," he said. "They blitz on first down about 35 percent of the time, and when they do, the linebackers are always in tight. When I came to the line I recognized the formation, so I looked over to Randy and signaled the fly pattern. I knew one on one they wouldn't stay with him, especially this late in the game—we had practiced that all week."

Take a minute and re-read that—look at all the preparation that went into that moment and think about how long that quarterback thought about that moment, lived that moment in practice, and practiced that moment. He was one of the few people on the field who was *not* living that moment for the first time in his life—he was reliving it! He had thought about that moment in his mind's eye; he had envisioned it to the point where he recognized it was the moment, and then he simply lived it again.

Like an athlete, a manager must always think about "the game"—the environment, goals, and vision.

This isn't a sports phenomenon, this is management. That quarterback managed the game and his team. As a manager, you must think constantly about your team, your environment, your goals, and your vision. You must think about the game. I find when I am reviewing a business or simply reviewing my monthly activity that has past or that has yet to come, I can envision what I want to have happen or happen differently.

I think about my business, I think about the situations that I will be in and that my team will be in, and I talk to them about those situations before they occur. We think through the responses, the actions, the discussions, and the reactions.

In 2004 I presented a budget to my new boss and his management team. My division was transferred over to him because the market was in a downturn, and the company decided we needed to downsize my division and expense manage it to a point of acceptability.

Our plan was a loss. The reality of our business was that the market had fallen off suddenly and dramatically, and we were left with downsizing expenses in the first quarter and a very weak revenue stream to cover any stress on the already-thin margins we had.

In addition, the portfolio of customers we had to service was acquired at incremental market share–related pricing, a decision that was made at the corporate level and that somehow had been forgotten! In any event, as I began to think about the budget and the plans we had, I realized the best we could do was to minimize the losses we would incur and downsize the business, but even then we would lose some money. As I thought about this moment, I began to envision what the conversation was going to be like. Being a new boss and a new member of an existing team and showing up with a planned loss did not bode well.

I decided that when the conversation got ugly—and I believed it would—I needed to stay focused on my business. I needed to stay positive and not get trapped in the emotion of the issues. I needed to embrace any advice and not get engaged in defending myself, but stay factual and confident in my plan, despite its financial disappointment. I truly felt that no one else could deliver a better plan.

The day came. I had prepared my team for a rough review, and I asked them not to panic or engage in any negative conversations that might occur. I also told them that I was fine with whatever happened at the meeting and that they should be prepared to see their boss on the firing line. I also told them something else—to watch and learn from this experience. I told them I would do well at times and make some mistakes, but they needed to learn something. That alone changed their mindset about the day—we were going to learn.

Finally, we prepared for the session by having a trial run, which was actually fun. We rehearsed the review, and they got a kick out of bashing and thrashing me—they were pretty good at it, too!

That day we walked into the room, and it was apparent that the review was going to take a bad turn. My new boss was at the head of the table, and his entire team sat on one side of the table, leaving a few empty chairs on one side of the table and a few chairs behind them.

He began the review with this statement: "I have read your plan, and maybe you can start by telling me why I shouldn't fire you." (True story!) There were about 20 people in the room, and to say you could hear a pin drop just doesn't adequately describe the situation—I would say you could hear people's hearts beating. Yeah, that sums it up all right....

In our rehearsal, as a joke one of my team playing the part of my new boss had opened our review with, "Tony, you are fired!" That had brought a big laugh at the rehearsal, and although I didn't respond to it at that moment, I thought about that as a possible opening—an opening that would have all my new peer group, all my direct reports, and my boss looking to me to respond. I thought and thought about it, and I responded in my mind a number of different times and reflected on each. I also had thought about similar but less demeaning types of openings, and all of them ran the same path in my mind. But what I ultimately chose to say was borne of the thought of how I would want *my* employee to respond to that comment.

Like that quarterback, I wasn't living this moment for the first time—they all were, but I had been here before in my mind's eye, and I had seen this all take place in my own vision of the day. So I was ready—more ready than anyone, including my boss!

I looked at him and said, "I think if you feel like that after we review this material, you should fire me. I want the best for this division and so do you—that's what matters. Who runs it is your decision, and I will respect whatever it is, but I would at least like the opportunity to present this plan to you."

He went from stunned to fighting back a smile; his team went from smirks to a wide-eyed, frightened look that I believe they simply exchanged with my side of the table. The review went great, and later my boss would say to me, "Tony, only you could have pulled that off." That's not really true, though—the real truth was that only someone who had prepared, only someone who had thought about it could have pulled it off.

Be Relentless

When I first started out in the business world, I worked for an oil company. The senior management was very involved in the business, and although revered, they were very approachable. One of the senior managers was respected as the best. He was the number-two guy, and everyone respected him and praised him. That said, he also was feared and known as a very tough guy. I was a young guy, and I did a lot of reports and special projects—mostly stuff no one wanted to do, long hours, travel, and tedious-type work.

The reward was the opportunity to interact with the top management. I would get the chance to pick their brains and maybe get some advice.

I was on a project for "Z" and it was rather late one night—I mean really late, like 11:00 p.m. Not only was it late, but it was in New York, and after 11:00 p.m. in New York, there are no buses that leave the Port Authority back to New Jersey, where I was living. This fact was pretty well known at that time. I was at my desk, which was out on the floor, but the angle was a straight shot into Z's office. He was there, desk lamp on, reading and calculating and making notes.

"Meola!" He barked my name like a bear growls, and he summoned me into his office. I went in, and believe me it was an awesome office—the big mahogany desk, the globe, the office lamp with the pull chain, the map of the world on the wall with all of our barges' and ships' positions marked with precision. I was in awe of the place, and I thought to myself, "This is going to be me someday!"

"What are you doing out there?" was his question, and I explained to him the project I was on and the work I was engaged in; I started telling him all about the project. He listened, asked a few questions, told me a few approaches I should take, and then asked how I was getting home to New Jersey. When I told him I planned on staying the night and finishing the project, he half laughed and told me he would drive me home—well, his driver would drive me home!

But I took the opportunity that was given to me, and I asked him questions I have asked executives and people of power all my life: "How did you get to where you are today? How did you become you? What do you have that others don't?" Over the years I have heard a lot of responses to those questions, but none was as confident and powerful as Z's. He didn't even think about it; it was as if he knew exactly why he was successful. He looked at me and said, "I am relentless." That's all he said—no explanation, no story about the time when he was young, no mention of a mentor, nothing...just "I am relentless." And actually, that was all he needed to say.

On the ride home, I asked the driver what it was like to work for Z the way he did. He smiled and said, "Oh, the stories I could tell you...," but he never did. He did say that Z worked every hour of every day and that there was nothing Z could not do. He said that Z wasn't the smartest executive he had driven or the best spoken, nor was he the best dresser or the calmest, but there was just something about him that you knew he wasn't going to fail at anything he did. I smiled and thought to myself, "Relentless!"

Choose your goal, belief, and passion, and then be relentless in pursuing it.

Over the years, I have gotten an appreciation of what that word really means. Webster's dictionary will tell you that it means persistent, unremitting. I have come to know it as simply being in tireless pursuit of a goal, being passionate and unwavering. But you cannot be relentless about everything in life and in your career, and that is the real lesson I learned. You need to choose the goal, choose the belief, and choose the passion—then and only then can you be relentless in your pursuit of it.

When I took over that little accounting unit I wrote about in Chapter 1, I was relentless in the pursuit of making that unit the best accounting unit in the company. I was constantly thinking about what we could do better, how we could become the best, and what we had to do differently. I committed myself and asked all those around me to commit to that goal. I told the others who could not commit to leave, and I meant it.

I sought out the opportunities, thought about the things that would make us better, and asked successful managers what they were doing to achieve their success. I worked and worked seven days a week, 24 hours a day toward that goal.

The funny thing is that when you achieve the goal, and people ask you how did it, and you tell them (because you think they really want to know so they can replicate it), they look at you like you are crazy. And then you see in their eyes that they lack something that would make them work as hard as you just explained you did, but you don't know what it is. Well, I can tell you—they are not relentless.

Know When to Engage

The strongest warriors are those that never have to fight. It's a simple saying, but it speaks volumes to the point of knowing when to engage in a situation and when not to. Sometimes not engaging in a situation is more powerful than actually being in the middle of it. As a manager you will be in situations every day where people will want to see your reaction, get you involved in conversation, and have you take action. And you should do all of that, provided you are prepared, have thought it out, and are comfortable, because as a manager that is your responsibility. You must be prepared, and when you are not, you are allowed to tell people that you need some time to think the issue through before you respond. That is what you are expected to do. What would you think of a manager who reached conclusions, made decisions, or reacted without thought and preparation?

> Sometimes not engaging can be the best course of action.

That is what people will think of you if that's how you choose to conduct your business as a manager. In addition to that, if you engage in a situation for which you are not prepared, then chances are you won't be very successful. It's the old card players' rule of knowing when to hold them and when to fold them.

I was in a business review in one of my first divisional jobs, and we had gotten to a point in the review of new business startups. We had prepared an analysis on going into the Utah market as one of three different new market propositions. My boss flipped open the tab in our binder that listed New Business Ventures Proposed and looked at the index, a modest page with just three markets listed on it:

- Pennsylvania

- Atlanta

- Utah

He announced, "Well, we don't need to talk about Utah, that's for sure. In 16 years, I have never been successful in that market, and that includes buying a company that was successful in the market there! I just don't know what it is about our company and that market that doesn't click."

You have the setup, so what did I say? "I think we have found the right formula this time, and after reviewing it with us, I am sure you will agree." I do not define this as engagement, but what followed was indeed engagement! My boss said, "Tony, with all due respect to you and your team, I am not interested in Utah. The market just isn't right for us, and our investment capital is limited and a scarce commodity for the shareholder, so we will pass on Utah." Then (and only then) was the point of engagement. He had said what he wanted to say, and I had said what I wanted to say, so to continue required some form of engagement by one of the parties. You get the point? I wish I had then, I can tell you that!

I engaged: "Honestly, if you give us a chance, I think we can convince you. I really do." What was I thinking here? I wonder that even as I am writing this story! Needless to say, he went on a bit of a rant, and we didn't talk about any investment strategy at all that day.

But I didn't really learn the lesson until about a week later. I was in his office for an unrelated issue, and he brought up the meeting. "Tony, we should talk a moment about the Utah thing. It wasn't about Utah at all; it was about you not respecting my judgment to the point of taking me on publicly over it. A better way to handle it would have been to approach me offline on it after I told you we weren't going to consider it. It was...well, it just was the wrong time."

That was the lesson in the nutshell—it was the wrong time. Remember when your parents were yelling at you when you were a kid, and they would say, "Did you really think you would get away with this?" They didn't want a response, and the fact is we all thought we would get away with it because that was part of the rationale to do it in the first place, wasn't it? But we didn't say, "Yes, I thought the plan was flawless and we would go undetected." We just stood there and didn't engage, right?

Many times in town halls, hallway walks, and even in the parking lot, employees will approach me and ask a question that is a bit out of context, and they will want an answer right then and there. In my early years as a manager, they sometimes would get one, and I would regret it. If you have an answer that is well thought out or that you have decided, then by all means respond, but if you haven't, just thank them for the question and tell them you will think about it and get back to them. People can and do respect that.

Often people just want to be heard, and there is no response required and hence no need to engage. I was conducting my staff meeting one day, and I gave the responsibility for reviewing all of our projects and priorities to one of my direct reports, Joe, and asked him to report back to the group with a recommended priority list. I asked him to work with all of the people in the organization who actually worked on the projects instead of our executive team around the table.

One of my directs was obviously very uncomfortable with that and said, "I don't think that is a good idea. Joe doesn't know all the details and objectives of all the projects, and he may not realize a project's true priority." Before I could say anything, Joe responded. "I think I know a lot more than you think I know. I will deal with it. I got it, Tony, no problem."

I let the conversation go on not for its entertainment value, but actually to make a point. "I disagree, Joe," my other direct, now leaning forward, repeated, as if the leaning was going to change something. "You can't possibly know everything there is about every project there is."

Now and only now was I ready to speak. "Well," I started, "that could be a problem that is beyond Joe. You see, no one—not even all of us combined—will know everything about every project there is to know, but I am thinking we probably can decide our priorities just shy of being all-knowing. I think we all expect Joe to review the projects and make a recommendation, and for us to have a collective discussion and reach a common goal on priorities. Can we agree on that?"

My dissenting direct report looked puzzled and said, "I can agree on that as long as that is the assignment." Before Joe could respond, others actually laughed to themselves a bit, and I said, "Agreed."

The coaching I gave the dissenter after the meeting was simple. He didn't trust Joe, period. That was the issue, he looked foolish trying to cloak the issue with the whole all-encompassing knowledge bit, and in the end he damaged his own credibility. What he should have done was ask Joe how he envisioned pulling off the assignment, and in doing so he would've had an opportunity to engage him in a positive way where he actually had some input.

My favorite example of engagement comes from my son's job. He worked in a country club as the food and beverage manager. A new boss was brought in to oversee the club, and in the first meeting the new boss asked what the team could do to increase sales and bookings.

The sales manager and my son were not on the best of terms for whatever reason, and she began to say the biggest issue for sales was that the food and beverage area was not running properly. Her example was that the popcorn machine was dirty. Now, let's face it—that was a pretty weak argument, and probably a simple, "We'll get it cleaned, no problem" would have sufficed. A "Hey, we will put that on the list, and I will lay out all the issues we need to fix, including the popcorn machine" would have been even stronger. Instead, what ensued was a staff meeting about a popcorn machine, how it gets dirty, why it is so tough to clean, and apparently its psychological impact on the sales manager that manifested itself in poor bookings.

So, the new manager had his first staff meeting at a struggling country club and discovered that the core of the entire place revolved around the popcorn machine. Not only did the manager waste everyone's time that morning, but the club was no better as a result of the meeting with the entire staff. You wonder what he thought of both the sales manager and my son as the conversation played out.... I do know what my son thought—he left the company and is a very successful manager in a restaurant now. Oh yeah, and they closed the country club.

In closing, these are the vital few lessons that I hold with me every day as I approach my role and the responsibilities I have today as a manager and a CEO.

1. Stay positive.
2. Think about it.
3. Be relentless.
4. Know when to engage.

Finally, I would like to share a philosophy of management that I think captures it all: Remember, first have a vision, then hire the right people. Select each one with the vision in mind, train them, give them the tools to succeed, and finally create the environment for them and for you to obtain that vision.

Appendix

Encore: A Picture Is Worth a Thousand Words

- #1: Decision Making
- #2: Capabilities and Success
- #3: Goal Clarity and Performance
- #4: Priority Management
- #5: Performance Change (the Checkmark Theory)

Over the years I drew many a picture as I explained management theories or made a point to my team—so much so that the napkins, scrap papers, and envelopes with these gems on them jokingly have become collector items by the many managers that I have encountered along the way. I thought it would be fun and useful to share a few of these charts of managerial life according to Meola!

#1: Decision Making

Time

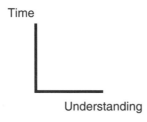

Understanding

Decisions are a function of time and understanding: The more time you have to make a decision, the greater your understanding of the decision points and the better your resulting decision.

That sounds simple enough, but putting it into practice is another story. When I am faced with a decision, the first thing I determine is how much time I have to make the decision. Once I know that, then I can determine my approach and speed of processing data in order to make the best decision I can given the amount of time. That is the problem people create in decision making—they do not understand the time factor. They think without time limits and often are not effective because they take too long or not long enough. They either didn't have the time to understand the issue, or they analyzed it beyond a point where more information added no value—the law of diminishing returns set in, and the decision opportunity passed them by.

I always use the example of a room on fire. If you were to tell me that the room I was in at this very moment would be on fire in the next three weeks, I can guarantee you that I would be safe and so would any possessions I have in this room. If you told me that it would be ablaze in three seconds, I can almost guarantee you that something would be lost. Same understanding, different time parameters.

Managers must make decisions—it's part of the job description and the pay grade. Typically, we gather data, analyze it, consider alternatives, and decide. The process never changes—that is decision making. What *does* change is the time you have to do that in. Consider the driver who is crossing an intersection when another car runs through the same intersection unexpectedly. The driver of the first car hits the brakes to attempt to slow down and give himself more reaction time, and then he turns left or right to avoid the collision.

Let's step through that again. The driver gathers data—an unexpected car has entered the intersection. The driver analyzes the data—there is going to be a crash unless I do something. The driver considers alternatives—turn left or right. And the driver decides—turn left. All of that happens within seconds, but the fact of the matter is that each stage *does* happen. So, too, it is in management.

When I was running a major division in the late '90s, the company I worked for acquired a similar company—actually, one of my division's major competitors. My boss asked me whether I was going to keep any of the management team of the company we were acquiring. In response, I asked him the question I always want to be clear on in decision-making situations: "How long do I have to decide?" His response was, "48 hours after we make the acquisition." With any acquisition, firms go through a due diligence period, a bid process, and then acquire. Knowing that I had to make that decision within 48 hours after we made the acquisition, I chose to go on the due diligence team and out on the due diligence visit. I interviewed the senior managers on that visit, sat in department reviews to understand how they ran their areas, and spent personal time with each one to assess the fit. Due diligence lasted six days.

Usually a manager at my level would not go on due diligence reviews, but I knew that I would not have sufficient time to make a good decision unless I changed the approach and gave myself more time. Having given myself additional time, I then began the process of increasing my understanding, and I ultimately made a very good decision on who would fit and who would not. If all I had was the 48 hours my boss described to me originally, I certainly would have gone through the same evaluation process, but the result might have been impacted by time.

I can recall a situation when I was a young manager that made the point to me about decisions being a function of time and understanding. I was a supervisor, and the human resources manager came to see me one day and informed me that one of my employees had stolen a company calculator from one of the accounting desks. It was back in the days of the old 10-key desktop calculators. The situation was not good, and the disciplinary action was clear—termination. But there was an additional problem: Another employee apparently saw this happen and did not say anything, and human resources wanted that employee terminated as well.

They had confirmed the allegation through a third employee who had come forward. My decision as a manager was whether to fire the employee who was there but did not say anything. All of this went down on a Friday afternoon—it was exactly 4:00 p.m. when human resources came to see me. She was very anxious and said, "We need to make this decision before these two guys go home." Being a young manager-stud, I of course was ready to fire anybody and everybody who violated company policy, so I did what I was supposed to do—I called my boss to let him know that I was going to fire two of the five accountants who worked for me.

It was an interesting call. He asked me a few questions. First, when did this theft go down? Answer: Last evening, when we had worked late. Second question, when did the model honest employee go to human resources and let them know what happened? Answer: 3 p.m.—and I added that human resources verified the calculator was indeed missing and verified in the sign-out log that all three employees left at the same time—8:05 p.m.! Man, I was good!

So then he asked me two last questions. He asked what kind of day I was having. I told him, "Busy." I was in project meetings most of the day and handled an emergency request for a reforecast of our sales numbers for the month. He then asked, "Why do we have to fire these guys today?" I said I didn't know, but I thought we should fire them. His response was simple, "Why today?" When I didn't have a really good reason for why today, he said I should do it Monday at 5 p.m., but keep everything we knew confidential and come up with a plan for how we would run the department down two people until we replaced them.

That Monday, I came in and was all set with my plan for how to move forward. I knew how I would conduct the termination meetings—and then the unthinkable happened. Guy number 2, the silent observer of theft, came into my office and asked if I had a moment. He proceeded to tell me how difficult of a decision he had to make in coming to me and that our employee had stolen the calculator. He explained that he was fearful of retaliation but could not let it go; he had to speak up, so he came to see me.

When I went to see my boss, I asked him how he knew this guy would come forward, and he said he really didn't, and in fact he didn't even think the guy would. He said his concern was how we would go forward and to make sure I had thought the plan through before we fired both of them. Then he said something that really resonated and gave me the seeds of my decision theory—he said, "Plus, this isn't a time-sensitive decision. You can fire them anytime you want once you have the facts locked up."

Now, granted, the facts changed, so we made a different decision. But I took away from that a different view: We didn't have all the facts, but what we *did* have was time, and we used it to get all the facts to make the best decision.

As you adopt this approach, you will get better and better at knowing when to pull the trigger on a decision because you will be aware that decisions are a function of time and understanding. You will get better at reaching understanding faster because you will develop methods in limited-time situations that you can use in longer-time decisions as well, and you then will have the luxury of reflecting on your decision before you have to make it.

#2: Capabilities and Success

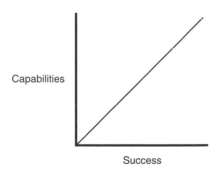

It seems to be common sense: The more capable you are to achieve your success, the more likely you are to be successful. You would think that this was rocket science, profound thinking, or the best-kept secret in the business world. Throughout my career, which has spanned some 30 years, I have seen countless projects, endeavors, and companies fall to failure because they did not understand this basic concept, and as a result they never managed it.

As a manager, before you place your organization into a position of pursuing the goals, undertaking the project, and participating in any situation in which it must deliver, you have to ask yourself a basic question: Are we capable of achieving this task? As the manager, you are responsible for the team's success, and that means you must position them for success by readying them for it.

This may mean you add a player, change a policy or a practice, set more time to review the details of the actions you are about to undertake, add outside help, change internal players, or do whatever it takes to answer the capability question—yes! And if your team (or you) is not capable, the question then is how do you (or can you) compensate for that fact?

Every manager has numerous projects and tasks to get done, and the tradeoff is always people and projects—not enough of the former and too many of the latter. The reason for that being a nearly universal truth in management is because most managers manage every project the same way, according to their project management process. Very few managers first assess the capability of the team and then say, "Based on this capability, here is how we will manage the project."

In every company I've managed later in my career, for every project I would carefully select the project team, assess their capability, and shore up the team so we could have a better chance of success. I can tell you this for a fact: This approach works. Team talent, chemistry, and knowledge produce capability.

As the year 2000 approached in business, the big focus and scare was whether our systems would work when the clock struck 12:01 a.m. on January 1st. I happened to be the COO of an organization in 1999, and as such, I ran the Technology department. I remember talking to my director of IT and asking him, "Do we have the appropriate talent to review and enhance our systems to ensure that the company will be up and running?" His initial response was, "Of course we do."

"Great," I said, "so what are the capabilities we need?" He looked at me like he was staring down the barrel of a loaded gun! He then began to free-think some of what we would need, and I stopped him as he struggled with the list: "Mark, go back and think this through in detail and then answer the question."

That year we used outsourcing, contract labor, joint departmental teams, and industry consultants and hired several key players to bring that team the talent it needed to be successful. And when January 1, 2000 came, we were up and running without incident. The team was prepared for the task at hand and delivered because we, as management, made sure they were capable.

Capability doesn't always deal with the technical aspects. I remember being faced with a management decision regarding whether we should buy a company that was in our industry and for sale. I was asked to put together a team that would help make this decision by reviewing the company and making a recommendation. I gathered my team and a few key members, and we visited the company.

As we met with people and reviewed the technical aspects of the company and how it was run, my head of human resources pulled me aside and made a comment to me. She said the culture of the company simply would not fit with our company's culture; they were a smaller organization with a parent-like culture, with very few documented policies and procedures. They ran more by trial and error than by process and procedure.

Had she not been on the team that day, we may have made a terrible mistake and tried to merge two companies that fundamentally would never be able to operate as one entity. The rest of my team was incapable of seeing the cultural distinction that she saw, but that is why I had her there in the first place—to advise me on the people aspects of the transaction.

Once you assess the capability, you know your gaps and then you adjust. I recall having a brilliant, talented team on a key project, but I knew this team had never worked together on any project before, and the learning curve of a team working together for the first time was something we didn't have a whole lot of time to deal with. The other aspects of a new team—no chemistry, lack of trust, and so on—all would be at play as well. The talent this particular team had was truly amazing; in fact, they all are very successful managers today in prominent positions.

To counterbalance this gap or weakness, I made sure we brought that team together more frequently than our project management process called for in review sessions. Sessions where they had to support each other and talk through the challenges they faced helped them come together as a team. Just the fact that they all had to come to headquarters and to my conference room forced them to bond; just the frequency of them being together caused the learning curve of dealing with each other to accelerate.

They succeeded in part because they overcame the obstacle of teamwork that is always present on a new team. At our first meeting on the project, I asked them how they would overcome this obstacle themselves, and they went to work on it. Many times they thanked me for bringing the obstacle to their attention and pointed out that the fact that I did helped them recognize and overcome it.

When running a department you can see that you need to build capability through training, process, technology, and policies that allow your people to achieve the task at hand. But young managers often simply dive in and begin fixing things, meeting, and conducting activities before they even realize that the mismatch of capabilities and success is, for the most part, what they are trying to overcome.

Capabilities and success go well beyond project management, although that is where I see the most frequent violation of the understanding of this principle. It applies to crisis management as well.

I ran a technology organization, and we had implemented a new payroll system. It was the second run of the payroll cycle, and I was sitting at my desk when the head of application and development came to see me. This wasn't just any payroll system—we had written this system in what was one of the latest languages of the day (Java), and we had also used some heavy calculation software (C++). We were pretty proud of the system; the capabilities were amazing, and it had several user interfaces that made managing payroll complexities, such as incentive compensation, draws, and holdbacks, a snap!

Testing had gone well; the very few issues were all taken care of, and we placed the system into production one month early. The first cycle was flawless. Things had gone well! Well until that morning, that is. That morning was payday. By the look on the application and development manager's face, something was not quite right. He said, "The payroll system locked up in production, and we can't figure out why." As a manager, nothing is scarier than when they tell you that there is a problem and they can't figure it out, because typically "they" are all you have!

I placed a call to the CEO and let him know the situation. He asked me to look into the issue and update him within the hour. I immediately called a meeting with my direct reports to discuss what had happen and how we needed to respond. Their suggestion was to form a taskforce and begin to analyze the solution. I called the meeting, locked up the people, and we began to figure this out.

About two hours into the session, my administrative assistant came to see me; my boss was on the phone. I stepped out. He asked where we were with the system. I told him I had a group of our IT folks locked up in a conference room. He then gave me a lesson in capabilities and success. He said, "Tony, these are the guys that got us in this mess in the first place! If they were capable, we wouldn't be here!"

When I hung up the phone, I called the Gartner group and IBM. Within four hours, we had experts on the phone, and a day later in the office. We resolved the issues, and the system was back up and running. The point was that Gartner and IBM consulting are in the business to solve problems. That is their core capability, whereas my team was not used to solving problems in crisis. They did not have a standard approach, tools, and so on that lent to the success factors.

The bottom line is that you always need to know where the capabilities of your team are—where they are weak, where they are strong, when you need to add strength, and how much time you need to direct and review. All this comes together in a formula for success when you manage capabilities.

#3: Goal Clarity and Performance

The better defined the goals, the better the performance and the more likely you are to achieve the goals. As a manager you define goals at all different levels. There are the goals of the organization, the goals of your direct reports, the goals of the business, and the goals of all the employees. But one thing is true: The clearer the goal, the more likely you are to achieve the result you are looking for.

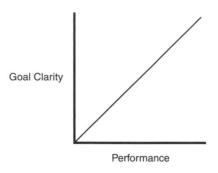

Goal Clarity

Performance

Clear goals are understood well enough that team members can perform the desired behaviors to achieve the outcome. Many managers complicate goals with sub-goals and specificity that they later regret. Remember, you want them to be understood well enough to achieve the desired behavior.

Suppose you want someone to answer the door when someone outside is trying to get in. You might have a goal that says, "Answer the door when the doorbell rings." Sound good to you? Here's my question: What if someone knocks? The clarity of the goal depends on what you are trying to create with the goal. In the door case here, you may only want the doorbell addressed. If that's the case, you have a good goal definition going. But if you want the door answered regardless of the method used by the entrant, then you may have some ambiguity playing into your equation.

Clarity is different than specificity, and that is a cardinal rule in setting goals. Consider the example of my cost-conscious manager, who met the cost goal but missed the point on the overall profit and loss picture. This happens all the time and is exacerbated when you tie the goals directly into compensation.

I ran an IT project a few years back—a pretty large-scale system implementation—and as always, my boss stood up in front of 3,000 people and made the executive blunder of committing to an implementation date that was very aggressive and about three months off what we could achieve. As a result, the date became the goal, and to meet the goal we had to cut back on the functionality the system would deliver—in the famous IT speak, "phase one."

We delivered on the date, but it was a disaster. The system didn't have a number of the originally promised functions, and people were upset and disappointed. The IT department felt terrible, as did the project team, because we all delivered an inferior product.

But it was all about the date and my boss's credibility. The reality is the goal was no longer to deliver a system to enable people to be better at their job; it was now to deliver a system by a date.

As with the change performance curve and the decision curve, these are theories that exist, and you cannot avoid them. But you can recognize and manage them accordingly, and as a manager, that is exactly what is expected of you.

So how does one manage goals and then performance in an integrated fashion? To begin with, you need to work at setting goals. Too many managers and even executives simply form goals that sound good, but then do not take the time to work out the goals to ensure that they will achieve the result and have the desired impact. Twice in my career, I took over organizations that were in a position where their future as a company was uncertain; in both cases the parent company was reviewing the organizations for sale. In both cases I sat with the management team that I had in place to run the organization and asked the question: "If you are running a company that is for sale, what is your goal?"

After hours of discussion about the outcomes of such a circumstance, in both cases we chose similar goals. The key vision or goal of both organizations was to create value. After all, if you are for sale, you want the market to pay the most it will pay for your company. If the buyer is paying over market value, chances are the employees and the organization that you run—the one the new buyer paid for—will be kept intact. After all, that is what they bought, and that is what they paid for.

In both cases, the organizations had goals around quality of execution, cost, and profitability that led to successful outcomes. In one case we sold the company for a record industry premium, and in the other we became an outsourcer. Our goals were all around creating value for sale.

If you want to deliver great customer service, your goals should come from what great customer service is all about. But be careful in goal setting, because for the most part, I have found you will get the exact behaviors you communicate as the ones you desire from your people. No one comes to work to be fired; rather, most people come to work to get promoted. Goals tell people what success is, so think to yourself, "If we achieve this goal, will we be successful? What are the instances where we achieve this goal but fail?" In those cases you will see other things that need to be addressed to converge your goals to success and bring clarity.

I spent my career in the mortgage business, where customer service, credit quality, price, and cost to produce all factor into the success of a company, along with volume of business or share.

When I ran the sales force, I recall having a goal session at the beginning of the year and discussing our goals. It was a critical discussion because our sales personnel did not receive salaries; their entire compensation was based on goals.

We began by saying that those people's goal was to book loans, so volume should be the goal of a sales force. Makes sense, right? They are the sales force. Then came the question of, if we achieve this goal, what would be the instance where we were not successful? The first thought was if the loans we generated did not result in a profit. So we added to volume a revenue goal for each salesperson to achieve and gave each salesperson an ability to have input into the price. We now had a goal that was revenue and volume based. Then the question again had to be asked, is this success? When you lend money to someone for 30 years, there is a bit of a tail on that transaction before you can declare success, but you can determine the credit quality of a loan up front, which will tell you in a predictive sense the likelihood of that customer paying you over the course of the loan. So, we added credit quality as a goal.

Fairly certain that we had a set of goals that made sense, we reviewed them again. Volume, revenue, credit quality—that felt pretty good, and then we thought it over again. Why would someone come to us for a loan? We added service levels. They had to be the best, of course—that is always what service levels have to be. One of the dilemmas we saw then was how much we should spend on being the best in service levels, so we added a cost goal as well.

Our goal was to produce long-term profitable market share by delivering superior service at efficient levels that allowed us to keep the customer's cost down and attract top credit-quality borrowers. We had specific goals to define that: Volume metrics, share targets, revenue targets, credit quality scores, customer survey data scores, and efficiency targets.

If we met those goals, we honestly could not fail; we could not think of an instance where if we hit these goals, the result would not be success. The discussions took about 12 hours and produced common and deep understandings for our team as to what the goals meant.

We then defined the rules of engagement around performance: how we would measure performance, when we would measure it, and when we would recognize it, reward it, and change it.

It is that type of clarity around goals that enables an organization to internalize them and create performance that achieves them.

#4: Priority Management

Important Not Urgent	Urgent Not Important
Neither Important nor Urgent	Important and Urgent

Every manager needs to manage a set of priorities, and somehow there are always more things to do than resources to do them. Throughout my career I have used many systems and have seen many different ways to prioritize. But perhaps the most effective way I ever managed and communicated priorities is by using this graphic.

All things we do as managers fall into one of these four quadrants. Think about it for a moment: There are things that are important, but they are not really urgent, meaning they are not time sensitive or critical. For example, you may have to submit a plan for your department in July, and if it is currently January, this is clearly an important thing to do, but it is not urgent, is it?

Then there are those things that are urgent but not really important, meaning they are very time sensitive but not really important. For example, you have to choose which airline you want to fly tomorrow morning, both flights are the same time, and you are in an aisle seat in coach either way—you need to make the decision, but very little is at stake.

There are those things that are both urgent and important. For example, you need to respond to your boss by noon about which bid you will recommend the company accept. Then, of course, there are some things that are neither urgent nor important to you. For example, you might be satisfied with your contract with a sales vendor, and he happens to be in town that day and wants to take you to lunch.

As you approach your daily work, there are decisions you must make—choices that every manager needs to make and does—but they can have very large-scale impacts. This methodology brings clarity to the allocation of time and energy you use in decision making, and it helps you line up your resources on the right projects and activities. It is important to note that this chart represents a point in time, and at times things move through the four quadrants in all directions, so it needs to be revisited at a frequency that depends on how fast your business moves, how fast you move, and what you are prioritizing.

I had the following list of projects to accomplish when I ran an IT division in our mortgage company in 1997.

A. Install a new operating system for the processing unit.

B. Fix the billing system, which continually went down and created duplicate billings.

C. Expand the scale of the phone system, because we exceeded our capacity from time to time, and it would busy out in our customer service department.

D. Hire a new head of IT. (Ours had just quit.)

E. Prepare a three-year plan for the IT department.

F. Choose a new vendor for the payroll system, because the contract would expire that November.

G. Submit potential dates for site visits for other IT departments during the year.

H. Decide which quarter I would host an executive town hall and submit to corporate events by Friday.

Using this priority management method, here is what I came to:

Important but not Urgent	E, F, D, A
Urgent and Important	B, C
Urgent not Important	H
Neither Urgent nor Important	G

That pretty much sorted out for me where I would spend my time the first week of January 1997; how much time, effort, and resources I would allocate to each of these tasks; and in what order.

Where this method is really helpful is when you have a set of priorities as a group, you have vision and a mission, and you need to sort out a list of what everyone wants to allocate resources to. You will find that this method pretty quickly separates out the relative importance of activities to a goal.

I ran a sales force in 2003, and as sales forces tend to do, this one had a huge list of things we needed to do to take advantage of the market—and, of course, a budget that was somewhat limited. They needed new products, new marketing materials, better pricing, more training, better compensation programs, more people in customer service, nicer facilities, better computers, and more giveaway items that I affectionately referred to as "trinkets and trash." In the planning session, where we had 28 sales managers in tables of four or five folks that had come up with these lists the day before, I sat and listened to each presentation for what we needed. The energy grew throughout the presentation to me. There were cheers at times, and folks were pumped up to tell the "big guy" what they really needed and see what he would do about it.

I approached the easel armed with a black marker and my method of prioritization. I asked the first question you must ask before you can add value in a situational activity: "What is our goal?" For a manager to successfully lead a team to an accomplishment, and for a team to successfully follow a manager to the same, you must agree on the goal. Remember, this was a sales force. It took no time at all for them to all say almost in unison, "More sales!"

"Great," I said in agreement. "Then I have the following question for you. Of all of these you have listed, what would you say is urgent and what would you say is important—something we *should* do—but not really urgent?" Stunned at first, as most groups are when I introduce this clever terminology and approach, they began a conversation, which evolved into a fairly heated debate and then an alignment on the things that were really important. The first thing they pondered was what the most important thing up there was—if they could only have one thing, what would it be? I smiled to myself because I knew where we were heading—

not the outcome by any means, but the path. It is a path that leads teams and managers to the correct focus.

"Pricing is key. We need better pricing; that is what the customer wants. Our pricing is just not competitive out there," said our manager from the Northeast division. He always was hung up on price, so that wasn't too surprising to me. Our manager from the Western region made an interesting observation: "I agree that price is important, but it is not *urgent* that we change it. We have done pretty well despite not being the low price and at times not being very competitive. I don't think if I had only one of these it would be price." That led to a robust discussion on price and how to deal with it, and also a conclusion: Price was important but not urgent.

My Midwest sales manager spoke next: "Well, you could cross nicer facilities off the list. That isn't critical for us. It would be nice, but nice isn't one of the categories." He was a bit of a reluctant realist—always pointing out reality but always apologizing for doing it! Everyone, including the manager who had raised it as an issue, agreed. That is the power of this concept—it forces perspective and alignment to a goal. Nicer facilities had gone from a must to neither important nor urgent in about 15 minutes. That created a mob-like mentality for a minute or two, and then the mantra was, "What else don't we need to waste our time on?" Another byproduct of this exercise and method is a laser focus that emerges on urgent items, with the rest falling off rapidly. You must be careful and mindful of those items you dismiss, and, as a manager, you want to keep them tucked away to visit now and then, but they fade rapidly.

Trinkets and trash and new computers fell into that category for these top sales folks who, only minutes before, desperately needed these same items to increase sales. They were now neither important nor urgent. Next up was a very lengthy conversation on new marketing materials, and the room was divided into important not urgent and, ironically, urgent but not important!

The group divided into two. The "urgent and important" team argued that our materials needed to be rewritten. They were old, stale, and too familiar to everyone out there. They didn't drive customers to us, so it was important and, yes, it was urgent to increase sales. The "urgent but not important" team agreed that we needed to refresh these materials as we started the year out in the market. It was time and they were stale, but they didn't feel it would increase sales if we did. The argument ensued, and the conclusion was as interesting to me as the argument itself had been. They concluded that we would not spend a great deal of time and money, but we would refresh the marketing material as quickly as we could before the selling season began.

Compensation is always a hot topic, but we had a very good plan and one that was competitive in the market, so that quickly fell into important but not urgent. It also was apparent to the team that more customer service people would be important, but the quality of the customer service people was really the driver to more sales, as was the quality of the salespeople we had. They quickly moved the idea of more people in customer service to important but not urgent and moved quality of all our people into urgent and important. They spent about 45 minutes talking about the quality of our sales force and how if we were known in the market for our product knowledge and helping borrowers select the right products, we would have a real advantage. Therefore, training made it to urgent and important. Then, for an additional 45 minutes, they spoke about the need to develop new products and to implement products that were available in the industry but not yet at our company. That went into the urgent and important category as well.

So our resources would be dedicated to two things in full gear: training and product development. That was where we would invest the best and most human capital and financial capital to realize more sales. We would refresh marketing materials so as not to fall behind or become stale, but we wouldn't go crazy there either. We would keep on the radar initiatives around compensation and watch and monitor pricing and staffing levels, but make no real investment or special efforts there.

And we would not update our computers, develop more and new giveaways, or upgrade our facilities, despite perhaps people who wanted to. We would be honest and tell them that it was not in the game plan for that year.

There you have it! That is just one of hundreds of examples that I can give you of the power of this tool and method to approach the development and prioritization of what is important and unimportant to your team's success.

Things that fall into the urgent and important category are your number-one items because they carry a timing with them that is condensed relative to everything else you have to get done. Those that are important but have relatively more time attached to their deadlines are indeed important, but they are not urgent. The most misunderstood category includes those things that are urgent but in the grand scheme may not be important to the goal, even though they need to be done.

Suppose you are having a meeting to discuss the marketing program. It is a big meeting with all your team, and you will determine the future of marketing. Pretty important stuff here. At the beginning of your meeting, right after you give your great welcome speech and outline the agenda and the goals for the meeting, your administrative assistant hands you a note that your boss wants you on a call at 10 a.m. with a group of managers and his boss to discuss a public relations release. He doesn't think it affects your division or people, and you don't have to prepare, but he wants you there just in case something comes up that may remotely impact you. So, what is that on this scale for you that day? Urgent, but not important!

Sometimes compliance and legal issues may fall into this area. To a company who does three percent of its business in Ohio, updating a system for new legislation passed at the state level in Ohio and must go into practice in seven days is urgent but not necessarily terribly important. They do not want to violate the law, but it is not important to their business—they could suspend business in Ohio and still have 97 percent of their business intact.

Of course, in all companies we fall into the trap of doing things that are daily routines that are neither urgent nor important to our goals by themselves. Perhaps you have a plant near your office or cubicle that your company put there, and vendors come in to take care of it. Someone manages that—they get billed, review the bill, pay the bill, argue the bill, send out bids, receive bids back, do the paperwork, and meet with the company. Is it important to your success as a company? Is it urgent? No, but you can argue some value to it...or maybe not. It certainly is not worth a great deal of time and energy or allocation of resources, because it is neither urgent nor important to the goal.

Over the years I have used this method to manage my personal calendar with my trusty admin! We will sit down and go over appointments, people that want to get on my calendar, meetings, projects, and so on, and we put the designation next to them. My admin then manages my calendar accordingly. I can't tell you what a powerful use of this application it is. My admin will come in and say, "The CFO wants to meet on the forecast. It is important but not urgent. When do you want to see him—Thursday?" That is the power of the grid in a nutshell.

#5: Performance Change (the Checkmark Theory)

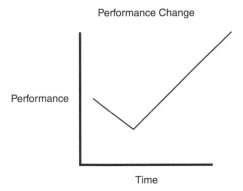

Change is one of the most used (and perhaps overused) words in corporate America today. There are so many aspects of change and managing change that you certainly can write an entire bookcase of books on the topic—and, in fact, we managers, authors, educators, and others have done just that! I certainly have a methodology and approach to change management that perhaps someday will allow me to join the plethora of experts on this topic, but to be a successful manager, one must understand the dynamic of performance change regardless of the method used to cause change.

There are two key factors of change that drive its performance dynamics. First, there is a learning curve involved in change. Second, every change is designed to work. Before you tell me that everyone knows that, consider how often the results of a change are underestimated or a change doesn't work the way it was supposed to. Also consider how often a change doesn't "take." I have been in many meetings in my life where the boss has said, "I thought we changed that."

The "checkmark theory" simply states that after every change, performance tends to drop off as the learning takes place and the expertise required to perfect the change begins to develop.

Managers must understand that the unit needs to make the adjustments that change demands, and that change itself takes time to master. Managers need to run the unit with that in mind—the unit needs time, care, and development support to make the change successfully.

As a manager, the second thing to remember is that most changes are designed to work. If you have ever found yourself reading assembly directions on Christmas morning and saying to yourself, "Okay, what are you supposed to do if it doesn't snap into place?" then you know what I am talking about. When the change doesn't go exactly as planned, it is usually because the mindset of the change has not been established well enough to carry the intent forward.

Similarly, when an individual performance change is occurring and there is a setback, the performer typically returns to the old behavior. The reason why is that the new behavior has not had time to become the new frame of reference.

As a manager, you need to monitor change very closely, and you need to inspect what you expect from the change to ensure that the new direction is developing forward.

In the mortgage business, one of the most feared parts of the cycle is the refinance boom. This is when rates drop, and the volume of mortgages begins to soar and overtakes the capacity of your team to process such volumes. It is a chaotic time even for the most experienced teams and companies, as the velocity of the volume stretches the operation's capabilities.

In 2003, I found myself putting in a major change to our processing platform. We had developed a team-oriented approach based on a high-performance workstation concept, new systems, and a "cradle to grave" approach to customer service. This had replaced the more conventional assembly line, handoff-driven process that the larger centers had run for years.

It was a major change that was about to be crushed by volumes the industry had never seen before. As we began the new process, we saw a slight dip in the productivity factors. People were learning the new process, but our first inclination was to start changing the already-changed process. This is exactly the point I am making when I say that rule one is that performance will drop off until the new process is learned and mastered. We began to change the process and lost the continuity of all the changes we had implemented. In a process change, all the changes are interdependent, and if you change one, you better understand what impacts it will have.

As the volumes kicked in, we had a problem. You see, the process called for incomplete applications to be cured by each customer service representative with their customer and sales representative, but there were so many applications that no one knew how to work the process when it was in backlog. So the units literally went back to the old process for backlogs, and in doing so, a new process spawned, but no one knew how to manage or track this new process. The result was chaos.

Two things had happened. One, we did not understand the performance dynamic of change and we overreacted. Two, when the activities exceeded what the process design would allow, we were lost because we did not design the process for the environment we were suddenly in—we designed it to work only one way! And if any other way was needed, we did not have the adequate alternative thought out. And if we'd had more time with the new process, the unit itself would have had the experience to flex the new process to change. But that was not the case, and, frankly, any process must contain alternative paths to address the second rule of performance change.

The same is true of an individual's performance. If you have an employee who is struggling with some aspect of his performance, you have a counseling session and agree on some changes he will make to his management style. The employee goes back into the line, and with the first crisis he encounters, he returns to his old style because he has no frame of reference built in the new style yet. He hasn't learned the new behavior yet.

So as a manager, what can you do to better manage performance change if this dynamic is truly the dynamic of change?

First, remember the curve—it is a checkmark. The newly changed situation will perform without noticeable change for the first cycle, then it will drop off somewhat as the learning curve begins to take place. As a manager, you need to make sure you are measuring the correct performance indicators in the process, and you need to inspect what you expect from a new process more frequently. Debrief daily and discuss what challenges the new process encounters and how the process is working. Any adjustments you may make need to be done holistically, with all implications thought through so as not to disrupt the process flows. Second, when you encounter unanticipated situations, you need to expand the design to accommodate these activities. That is the value of frequent inspections of the process in the beginning stages.

The exact same is true of someone you are coaching. I had a manager who was struggling with a new department she had inherited. The supervisor was resisting the change, and my manager was having trouble dealing with the situation. We discussed it and came up with a plan to deal with it. Again, the checkmark comes into play. I told her nothing would change immediately, but over the first 30 days we expected to see some change.

I would check in with her every two or three days, and we would discuss how things were going—inspect what you expect. We would adjust as we went. I am happy to tell you that the new manager finally succeeded in the transition, and they were a formidable team.

Don't be fooled by the performance dynamic. If you took over as commander of a naval battleship with no experience or training in the middle of a war, the ship would run as normal for some period of time, but it would slowly and perhaps unnoticeably (at first) deteriorate (the checkmark). When you are the replacement for a leader, remember this: For the first 90 days you are running someone else's organization. Also, remember as you begin to take control that the performance curve will dictate deterioration as people are learning your style. In the first few months, this is why things do not improve as rapidly as you think they will.

Frequently inspecting what you are trying to get done, discussing your goals, and making sure your messages sent are the messages received are critical to the process. In short, inspect what you expect with greater frequency and open discussion for the change to take and the upward slope to begin.

As with any management change, understanding the curve is the first step in managing the change successfully. Know what to expect, be aware of it, and plot your change on the curve over time and then ensure you pass through the curve to success.

Index

F

facilities issues, 40
feedback, 69, 89. *See also* **commu-**
　nications
　giving, 118–119
　importance of, 117–118
fields, binary, 76
finance committees, 146
firing, 86
floor meetings, 129
focus groups, 41, 83–88
　expense management, 165
　structure of, 88
formula of change, 72–73
frequency, management process,
　109–112

G

gathering data, 8
goals
　achievement of, 47
　attainable, setting, 121–122
　developmental, 89
　managing, 3
　obstacles, understanding, 31
　performance, 121
　tracking, 130
Good to Great, **62**
Google, 90
groups
　focus. *See* focus groups
　support, 112

H

hero managing, 41, 83
hiring, 86
honesty, 18. *See also* **values**
horizontal management systems,
　54–55
human resources, 9, 146

I

IBM help desk, 46
immediate issues, identifying,
　39–43
implementation, management
　process, 100–105
Industrial Revolution, 47
initial objectives, establishing,
　36–53
initiatives, management, 165
inputs, data analysis, 4
internalization, 66
Internet, 27
　blogs, 90
　communications, 95–96
interviews, 8
investment in tools, 5
issues, identifying, 39–43

J

Jordan, Michael, 174
junior underwriters, 78

K

key drivers of results, 101

L

languages, values as, 18
leadership
　management. *See* management
　personal value systems, 3
lines, starting, 39
Lotus 1-2-3, 45

M

macros, 45
mailing newsletters, 89
management, 3
  asks, 146–149
  commitment to vision statements, 11
  communications. *See* communications
  components, necessary, 16
  conflict resolution, 69–71
  definition of, 174
  environments. *See* environments
  expenses. *See* expense management
  focus groups, 41, 83
  Meola rule of, 170
  performance. *See also* performance
  reviews, 142–146
  surveys, 8
  values, synching, 21–31
management process, 97, 98
  committees, 113–114
  communications, 106
  depth, 109–112
  frequency, 109–112
  implementing, 100–105
  importance of, 98–100
  performance, 104–105
  success of, 105–109
management systems, 34
  change, articulating need for, 63
  horizontal, 54–55
  initial objectives, establishing, 36–53
  obstacles, 55–59
  organization of, 43–53
  planning, 53–54
  teams, assessing, 34–36
managers, roles as, 24
maps, processes, 100
markets, research, 14–15
McCartney, Paul, 69

measurements, 101–104
  capabilities, 121–122
  expense management, 169–171
  frequency and depth, 109–112
meetings
  brown-bag lunches, 91–92
  chart plots, 111
  corporate meeting pyramids, 113
  daily, 43–44
  floor, 129
  focus groups, 88. *See also* focus groups
  performance, 117
  positive attitudes, 176
  staff, 44, 70, 129
  staff, presentations, 149–151
  touch-base, 118
  town hall, 92–94
  town hall, presentations, 152–153
Meola rule of management, 170
metrics, 89, 101–104
mission statements
  developing, 14
  environments, adapting to reflect, 128–130
  evolution of, 48
  writing, 11–16
modeling
  behavior, 71
  change, 68–69
monthly business reviews, 142
monthly newsletters, 89–91
multiple responsibilities, 52

N

navigating obstacles, 55–59
need for change, articulating, 63–65
negative feedback, 117. *See also* **feedback**
news, Internet announcements, 95–96
newsletters, monthly, 89–91
nonnegotiable values, 28
notes, taking, 88

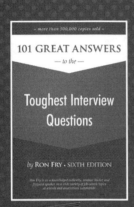
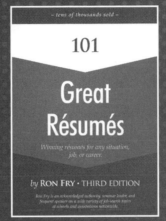

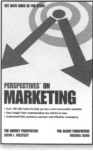